THE HOUSEKEEPER'S DIARY
CHARLES AND DIANA BEFORE THE BREAKUP

The Housekeeper's Diary

CHARLES *and* DIANA BEFORE THE BREAKUP

Wendy Berry

BARRICADE BOOKS INC.
NEW YORK

Published by Barricade Books Inc.
150 Fifth Avenue
New York, NY 10011

Printed in the United States of America.

Library of Congress Cataloging-in-Publication Data

Berry, Wendy.
    The housekeeper's diary: Charles and Diana before the breakup / Wendy Berry.
        p.   cm.
        ISBN 1-56980-057-X
        1. Charles, Prince of Wales, 1948–   —Marriage. 2. Marriages of royalty and nobility—Great Britain—History—20th century. 3. Women—domestics—England—Highgrove—Diaries. 4. Diana, Princess of Wales, 1961–   —Marriage. 5. Princes—Great Britain—Biography. 6. Princesses—Great Britain—Biography. 7. Highgrove (England)—Biography. 8. Berry, Wendy—Diaries. I. Title.
DA591.A33B47 1996
941.085'8'0922—dc20   95-9570
                                                                                        CIP

Fourth printing

The book you are about to read was banned in England. According to British law, no person who works for the Royal family may write about his or her experience.

In the United States, we are blessed with our First Amendment to the Constitution which guarantees freedom of speech and of the press. And so we are delighted to present Wendy Berry's thoughts and observations from the diary she wrote during her employment.

In the interest of publishing this book as quickly as possible and offering the reader an insider's look into what goes on in the Royal household, we are publishing it exactly as it came to us.

That means no changes have been made to the text; nor have spellings been "Americanized" or certain English expressions altered.

CONTENTS

1985

CHAPTER ONE

Love Alert

His Royal Highness Prince Charles Philip Arthur George Windsor, Prince of Wales, Earl of Chester, Duke of Cornwall, Duke of Rothesay, Earl of Carrick, Baron of Renfrew, Lord of the Isles and Prince and Great Steward of Scotland, and his wife were having an early night.

Just a few minutes before 10.30pm, the pair were lying, unusually for them, in the same bed in their elegant country home. Within minutes Diana had pulled off her long white T-shirt . . . their kisses grew more intimate. Both giggled as, in the throes of passion, Princess Diana with her foot knocked over a framed photograph of Althorp, her family home, on the bedside table. Diana stretched out her long legs, one foot now resting on the small wooden table.

Suddenly the door flew open and two police detectives, guns drawn, burst in.

'What the bloody hell do you think you are doing?' shouted Charles as he struggled to pull the sheets over him and his wife. 'Get out of here – at once!' As the embarrassed policemen made a quick retreat, the Prince grabbed a thick dark-blue towelling robe bearing his crest and followed them out on to the first-floor landing at Highgrove. 'You had better bloody well explain, and fast,' he barked. In low, apologetic tones, the detectives pointed out what had happened. Their explanation was met with a roar of laughter from the Prince.

Shortly after knocking over the photograph, Diana's foot had pressed one of the emergency buttons that are installed just a few inches away from every royal bed. She would not have realised what she had done, for the alarm doesn't sound in the room itself, only in the police post to the side of the house. On hearing it the detectives had immediately gone into emergency procedure. Two had raced towards the bedroom, while others radioed out for reinforcements. The heir to the throne was in danger . . . .

The story, in all its hilarious detail, was recounted to me shortly after I started work as housekeeper at Highgrove in November 1985. The entire episode was hushed up, of course, to avoid any publicity, but it was the topic of conversation for many months.

Highgrove security was necessarily extremely tight. There were panic buttons in every room, and sometimes more than one. In fact, in the early days staff often pressed them by mistake when they were dusting and cleaning. Though rather cumbersome in shape – they are solid, flat squares of gold-coloured metal with a little red button in the centre – the alarms certainly do their job. The squad is trained for moments like this, so within seconds Charles and Diana were surrounded!

Even though it was night-time there were apparently some very red faces. After all, it's not everyone who catches a naked Prince Charles on top of the Princess in the middle of making love.

Although the 'love alert' went into the annals of Highgrove staff legend, during my time as housekeeper I was never to see or even hear of such intimacy again. At least, not between the Prince and Princess.

.   .   .

Highgrove is a lovely house and should have been a very happy family home. The Prince and Princess regarded it as their country retreat where they could relax after a busy week, and in my first few years there they came for most weekends.

Both were devoted to their young family, William and Harry, and like any couple had their ups and downs. But apart from the occasional flare-ups they were substantially contented together when I first started in the winter of 1985, despite the occasional tears and scenes from the Princess. These outbursts were a sad foretaste of the marital agony the Prince and Princess, and by association their staff, were to live through over the next eight years.

I had been through my own domestic problems, divorced and left to raise four boys, but I still used to wonder what had gone so wrong between the Prince and his wife. Slowly, over the years, we began to realise that the marriage was under pressure, and that the Prince was pursuing his bachelor lifestyle. But right up until the early 1990s it seemed inconceivable that they could separate or divorce, so the only alternative was for them to swallow some pride and try to work their way through their difficulties as best they could. At least, that was what most of us thought.

Both had individual, fully absorbing activities at Highgrove in the early years: Charles his garden and Diana the young boys. Days were easily filled, occupied by the separate interests taken up by the couple.

There did exist a certain tension between them, and it was quite obvious that at times they simply did not get on, but generally the Prince and Princess would sustain civility towards each other, Diana referring to Charles as 'my hubby', and the Prince always calling her 'darling'. Both tried hard to be polite, especially in front of their guests. But in the later years even that was not always guaranteed.

Diana was incapable of hiding her true feelings for very long, and could be positively beastly to her personal staff. Tears were not just reserved for her, either, when things got a bit too much. She had a reputation for bringing about resignations by freezing people out of her circle, and was capable of making the lives of her personal staff a misery.

The sweet, kind-hearted, compassionate Diana is just part of a much more complicated whole. The part the public do not see is sometimes far removed from the 'Princess Act' – and none too pleasant. And because she was so riddled with insecurities and inadequacies it made her a very mercurial person to deal with. Quite frankly, one never really knew where one stood with her, or how she was going to react – unlike Charles, who, though extremely up and down in terms of temper tantrums, was generally straight and fair with his employees. However, when he did want changes made, nothing could dissuade him, and he could be extremely intransigent and ruthless. As long as he got his own way everything ran smoothly, but nobody could honestly say that he is an easy man to live with.

All of us were naturally drilled not to gossip about Charles and Diana's problems to anyone, and after a while the excuses became second nature. In fact, Highgrove and Kensington Palace staff even grew, albeit reluctantly, to accept the situation, dismissing the terrible rows and scenes as part of any royal marriage. However, unhappiness tends to breed unhappiness, and the couple's problems were capable of poisoning the atmosphere of the whole house.

Everything was fine as long as the staff put on a united front. In fact, the camaraderie in the face of adversity created a strong bond between us, and was only challenged later when staff were impelled to support either the Prince or the Princess. It was not an easy decision for anyone to make, since our livelihoods depended on our work, but it was forced upon us by their increasingly separate lives.

The first question for anyone who came on duty in the morning would be 'What mood are they in?' Depending on what the valet or dresser said, we would know whether we were in for a peaceful time, or for, as former Highgrove butler Paul Burrell would dub them, 'storm stations'.

Of course, I had been told what to expect by my eldest son, James, and his friends, who had worked for the Household at Buckingham and Kensington palaces before me. They all knew about Diana's eating problems, her terrible insecurities and her mood swings. They also knew how difficult and bloody-minded Charles could be when he didn't get his own way. But I dismissed the scare stories as simple exaggeration, because everyone seemed to thrive on the excitement of royal service. I entered as an innocent, deciding that until I had actually seen what it was like on the inside I would refrain from making judgements.

I remember James telling me about his initiation into the Royal Household. On his arrival at Aberdeen station in the late summer of 1982, he had been apprehensive. The excitement of getting a job as a footman had suddenly turned to panic as he realised what lay in store throughout the next six weeks at Balmoral – looking after the Queen, Prince Philip and the rest of the Royal Family. As the new boy, however, he was broken in very gently.

Dinner that first evening was an informal affair for the Queen, Prince Philip, an equerry and a lady-in-waiting. 'It was my first glimpse of the Royal Family at home,' said James, 'and to be quite frank my initial reaction was total shock. That first sight of the Royals sitting down at table chatting about commonplace things such as the day's walking and riding was unremarkable, of course. What was remarkable was the number of staff – the footmen, butler, Queen's page, cooks, pastry chefs and cellar staff all waiting on their every whim.'

He continued: 'I remember thinking at the time that it was that scene which stirred some hitherto unrecognised republican thoughts in my brain. It would not be too strong to say I was flabbergasted by all the staff required by just four people. The pastry chefs were on hand, for example, because one of the group had mentioned they wanted some bread-and-butter pudding for dessert. All the kitchen staff naturally stayed on duty to make sure this was produced at the right time at exactly the right temperature. It was an eye-opener, and there was one maxim I would never forget: four staff can always do a job better than one.'

. . .

By the autumn of 1985 I was in need of a job that provided my four children and me with some sort of security. In 1979 my marriage had fallen apart, and I went back to college, passing six O and two A levels in two years. After a three-year course at St Catherine's College, part of Liverpool University, I graduated with a BA in English, and by 1981 I was teaching A level English part-time, as well as English as a Foreign Language to businessmen when I could fit it in.

Home was in Formby, near Liverpool, a comfortable house, but we were constantly financially stretched. I knew that I needed something fixed and more secure. So when my son James mentioned that there was a housekeeper's job available at Highgrove, I jumped at the chance.

James had worked at the Palace as a footman, then as valet to both Princes Andrew and Edward. When he moved over to Kensington Palace he was in regular contact with Princess Diana. He had first met her at Balmoral, when he pulled off a social coup that was to stun many of his fellow footmen. He told me, 'All the royals, staff and many of the locals were invited each year to the Gillies' Ball. The Queen and Queen Mother absolutely adored the occasion, joining in with all the reels and other types of Scottish dancing.'

James and many of the other staff were still in livery after coming straight on to the ball from their duties. So it was a James Berry in uniform whom Diana confronted as the music started. 'One minute I was chatting with one of the footmen, the next minute this clearing had opened up in front of me, like some Biblical parting of the sea,' he laughed. 'There in front of me was a very pale, slim, beautiful Princess of Wales dressed in a long white ballgown. "You are James, the new footman, aren't you?" said Diana quietly. "Would you like to dance?"

'I put my drink down and rather self-consciously took her hand. The other men I had been drinking with looked on in amazement. Everyone secretly hopes and half-dreads they will be asked, but I think some were a bit put out that after years it had still not happened to them. The first dance was dreadful, on my part – I can't remember the number of times I trod on her toes, or spun her the wrong way. It was with relief that I heard the music come to an end, but just as I was about to suggest walking off the floor, she joked, "Not so soon, James, one more if you please." We both laughed and relaxed after that. We didn't talk on that occasion but there was some rapport. We were close in age, and over the years I was to become, like several others of her staff, increasingly drawn into her confidence.'

One afternoon in early September 1985 Diana and James were having a chat on the first-floor corridor of Kensington Palace. James, then under-butler to Harold Brown, had taken some tea through to her sitting room. Diana was describing the latest 'simply brilliant' Andrew Lloyd Webber show when she mentioned that she and the Prince were looking for a housekeeper at Highgrove.

'It's very difficult, James, because we can't advertise, but I thought you might know somebody,' she said. James said he would ask around – jobs like these are usually found by word of mouth – before she added with a dismissive laugh: 'I can honestly say I don't envy anyone the position. It's constantly raining there and Highgrove can be such a chore. The thing is that the children enjoy it, and I go because of them. It's important they can have somewhere like that to go at weekends.'

Just as she was turning to go James mentioned my name. She knew who I was – I had spent a week with him at Balmoral in 1983 – and she knew I had met and got on with several of the other staff, including Charles's valet Michael Fawcett, and Paul and Maria Burrell who were later to join me at Highgrove. 'Are you sure your mother would be interested, James?' she asked, cocking her head to one side. 'If she really is, tell her to write to Lieutenant-Colonel Creasy and fix up an interview.'

Four days after sending my letter to Colonel Creasy, the Comptroller of the Household, I was invited to London for an interview on Monday October 14. It seems that Diana had already spoken to him, because the letter made the interview sound a mere formality.

I bought a new blue suit and took the train down from Southport to London, arriving in a state of panic since we were delayed for half an hour. I was more than twenty minutes late for the 10am appointment, and for one terrible moment I wasn't sure if I should even bother going ahead with it. However, having decided there was nothing to lose I went to the side gate of Buckingham Palace and was led, still in a state of extreme agitation, to Colonel Creasy's office.

Inside, the extremely urbane soldier offered me a cigarette. I hesitated at first because I knew it was meant to be a non-smoking household. The Colonel, a tall, plump man in his early forties, read my mind. 'Don't worry, Mrs Berry,' he said kindly as he took out a packet of cigarettes. 'It's not a test. I smoke as well.'

He went through my CV. 'You are far too well qualified for anything like this, you know,' he said. 'But the Princess has told me that if you want the job then I am to give it to you. And if that's what she wants then I am in no position to go against her. By the way, she would like to see you in a minute, if that is all right with you.'

Amazed at the informality of the interview, I was shown down to the Palace courtyard, where I was met by the Prince's chauffeur Tim Williams in a maroon Scorpio car. He whisked me over to Kensington Palace and dropped me at the side door. It was opened by Harold Brown, the butler at Kensington Palace.

'Hello, Wendy, how are you,' he said warmly as he led me inside. 'Welcome to KP.' Harold, a career courtier, was dressed in a dark blue blazer with the Prince of Wales feathers motif on its gold buttons. 'The Princess is on the phone at the moment,' he added. 'So we have just enough time for a cup of tea.'

I don't know how I had expected a butler to speak, but I was rather surprised and impressed by the informality of this pale-faced and obviously terribly efficient man. I was later to hear that Harold, who was said to be a member of the strict Plymouth Brethren sect, could turn his hand to most things, whether making curtains or knocking out a set of shelves for the servants' quarters. Unlike several rather bumptious and pretentious footmen with ridiculous airs and graces, Harold was straightforward and very reassuring.

As he chatted away about Highgrove, he led me through to the butler's pantry, to the right of the main door. Passing a fridge in the hall, I was struck at how all the staff areas resembled the rooms of a rather dilapidated public school. There was a small flight of stairs that led up to the first-floor kitchen. A faint smell of toast and milk hung in the air.

Standing on the stairs in the royal part of the house, waiting to see the Princess, I was gripped once again by a terrible attack of nerves. Would she like me? What would she say? Would I be able to speak sensibly? It was, after all, the first time I had met her.

'Don't be nervous. She really is very sweet,' said Harold, squeezing my arm as he went to announce my arrival. 'And remember, call her Your Royal Highness first of all, then Mam to rhyme with spam after that.' I was ushered into her sitting room and saw her standing by the fireplace lined with invitations and family photographs. The door shut behind me.

'Now, you must be Wendy,' she smiled as she reached out her hand. 'I have heard so much about you from James. Come and sit down.' Standing in front of me was the most stunning-looking woman, in her early twenties. She was wearing a simple summer dress and looked at me for a moment with large, deep blue, smiling eyes. Her skin was perfect, her poise exquisite, the whole effect quite breathtaking.

Yet there was something about her, something that none of the many thousands of pictures taken of her ever really captured. It was her weight: she looked so much thinner than I had expected. As she turned and beckoned me to a chair I noticed how painfully fragile her back looked – her shoulder-blades visibly poking out through her silk dress.

'Now, I am so glad you want to work for us at Highgrove,' she said in her rather flat, Sloaney voice. 'But first there are several things you must know before you start, if you are still sure you want to. One thing you must realise is that it is extremely wet in Gloucestershire. In fact, it seems to rain all the time. Do you think you can cope with that? It's a wonderful place for the boys and my husband with all its outdoor things, but I'm afraid not really my cup of tea. If you are into country pursuits, however, you will love it.'

Diana explained in broad outline what my duties would include. 'We always have lots of log fires, so I am afraid these need to be cleaned every day. There is also quite a lot of entertaining and general day-to-day household administration, including preparing the guest rooms, which I am sure you are more than capable of. The Lodge at the end of the drive will be yours to use, of course, and since it is by the main road you might want to have it double-glazed. Apart from that and the damp, you might quite like it. I do think, however, you should go up there with Colonel Creasy to have a look around before you finally make up your mind.'

The interview lasted just a quarter of an hour, and I was struck by how beautiful and natural she was. I was charmed and made to feel comfortable. It was my first taste of Diana's charm, a formidable and potent force – and a force she would use in the future with devastating effect.

With a smile and another hand-shake Diana stood up and rang the butler's bell in the corner of the room. Harold took me downstairs to the drive where the Colonel and Tim Williams were waiting for me in the Scorpio. 'All right?' asked the Comptroller cheerily. 'We will head off up to Highgrove now, and stop for a bite of lunch on the way.'

We pulled in at a motorway service area. The Comptroller paid for everything and sat with me at one of the smoking tables. Tim Williams sat elsewhere. That apparently was the normal way of doing things in the Palace pecking order. As Comptroller, Colonel Creasy was an important man in the Household. As a housekeeper designate I appeared to be at a higher level than a chauffeur.

None of these things is ever written down. They are just known and understood. Newcomers therefore are faced with a veritable mine-field of potential gaffes until they start to pick up the workings of the hierarchy. Working for the royals, perhaps the most class-ridden organisation in the world, generates a similar class system among those in their service. In this way, Prince Charles's valet will always be deemed more important and powerful than his counterpart who works for Prince Andrew; the nanny to Prince William more revered than the nanny to Princess Beatrice.

Later that afternoon we approached Highgrove, in the tiny hamlet of Doughton, by a side gate, and were waved through by the policeman, who recognised Tim Williams and the car. We pulled up in the back courtyard and paused for a moment to look at the outside of the house.

Bought in August 1980 for over £750,000 from the Conservative MP Maurice Macmillan, Highgrove House was and continues to be Prince Charles's pride and joy. Set, when he bought it, in 347 acres of prime Gloucestershire land, Highgrove is less than eight miles from Princess Anne's house, Gatcombe Park, and not far from Badminton. Its extensive parkland also lies within the Duke of Beaufort's Hunt, a principal factor when Charles asked the Duchy of Cornwall to look into acquiring it. Originally built between 1796 and 1798, the house was heavily restored in the late nineteenth century after being destroyed by fire. An easy 120-mile journey from Buckingham Palace, it lay a mere seventeen miles from the home, at that time, of Camilla and Andrew Parker Bowles at Allington, near Chippenham.

Camilla was a regular visitor to Highgrove before and throughout the Prince's marriage to Diana. In the early days she had even lent the Prince her regular cook when he stayed at his country house. Highgrove's proximity to Allington was not lost on Diana, who just weeks after their engagement tried to persuade Charles to look for another country home. Her entreaties, however, fell on deaf ears and even caused anger when the subject was raised again, for the Prince was livid that anyone should question his motives or his movements as far as Highgrove was concerned.

Colonel Creasy rang the back door bell and we all walked in. There was no butler or footman to greet us, which the Colonel said was being looked into, since the Prince had informed his staff that both he and the Princess intended to spend more time there.

Inside, my first impressions were that Highgrove had had a lot of money spent on it and the rooms were immaculate. The Comptroller and Nesta Whiteland, then the housekeeper, who was suffering from lung cancer, followed us through and sat and chatted in the staff dining room. I looked at the drab beige walls there, badly in need of a paint job, and cast my eye over the wicker chairs and tables that had come from Diana's flat in Coleherne Court, which she had had before her marriage.

Joan Bodman, Nesta's live-out help, led me into the kitchen with its big deal table in the centre and showed me the large blue Aga used for all the house cooking alongside a double electric cooker and grill. There was also a large split-level cooker, and a microwave as well. We walked through the main kitchen and into the butler's pantry with the telephone exchange, where most of the calls apart from those on the Prince's and Princess's private lines were taken. Then, coughing nervously, Joan guided me through the main hallway, pointing out the dining, sitting and drawing rooms and the Prince's study.

Although the royals were not in residence I couldn't believe the state of Charles's study. Piles of loose papers were scattered all over the floor, opened books lay on the chairs and heaps of magazines lay dotted around like islands in some enormous ocean. 'Don't move anything in here,' laughed Joan. 'If a pen is on the floor, hoover around it.' There were many times later on when I used to split my skirt as I tried to step over the piles of books and papers.

As we climbed the stairs to the first floor I was told that only I, the valet and the dresser would have access to the Prince's and Princess's bedrooms. The butlers were under orders not to enter the royal rooms, which were the valet's territory and jealously guarded.

My look of surprise that the Prince and Princess had separate rooms led to a mysterious answer. 'Yes, that's right. You will soon see what's going on.' I let the matter drop, but just popped my head inside the two rooms, devoid of the personal belongings that travel with Charles and Diana wherever they are staying. 'The rooms need to be kept in a perpetual state of readiness in case one of them decides to graciously drop in at the last moment,' Joan added with heavy sarcasm.

Diana's room had a big sofa filled with cuddly toys including large Koala bears, a felt frog, a couple of giant penguins, teddy bears and a wombat. We walked through to her bathroom, which had fitted cupboards and a kidney-shaped table with photographs under its glass top. Another chest of drawers was covered with yet more ornaments collected on her travels. 'Any surface will be completely covered with her bits and pieces,' warned Joan. 'She likes all her knick-knacks around her.' My eye was caught by all the photographs of Diana and her family, in quite standard leather, wood and china frames.

Another flight of stairs and we were on the nursery floor, where Harry's cot was still up and ready for use. 'You will have to change Nanny's and William's beds and also be responsible for the other royal and guest bedrooms,' she explained. The nanny then was Barbara Barnes, and some of her odds and ends were laid out neatly on her bedside table. The day nursery itself was absolutely enormous, with a big cupboard full of toys, Lego and box games at one end.

Shortly before I left to have a look at the Lodge I was introduced to Nesta's husband Paddy Whiteland, Charles's groom and general factotum. He shuffled into the kitchen in old cords stinking of horses, and held out a very grimy hand. I liked him immediately, but could already tell there was a roguish side to his personality.

Over the next few years I learned a lot about Paddy and his special relationship with the Prince – the secrets and the trust between them. But for the time being I was confronted by a blunt-speaking Irishman who could do what he liked when he wanted at Highgrove, as far as Prince Charles was concerned. He laughed when I said I had worked as an actress and a teacher, and said: 'Well, you'll find a lot to learn here, if you come.'

Down at the Lodge, built in 1798, I was amazed to see a top-of-the-range fitted kitchen in what was after all only staff quarters. If anything it had better units than those in the main house. 'Wedding presents,' laughed Colonel Creasy. 'In the end we had so many of the ruddy things we didn't know where to put them. There's one in the valet Ken Stronach's cottage as well.'

On the way back to London I told the Colonel I would take the job. 'Magnificent,' he exclaimed. 'I hoped you would. Incidentally, the pay is £5,600 a year, you will need your own car and you can start on November 1.'

CHAPTER TWO

Early Days

'Hello there, you must be Wendy. Would you mind getting a bucket and sponge ready? Harry has been sick in the car.'

Such was my auspicious first meeting with Prince Charles. It was an early Friday evening in November 1985 and he had just arrived from London with his detective Colin Trimming in the chauffeur-driven Bentley. Diana and the boys were in the stretch Ford limousine, followed by the police back-up. Both were due to arrive quite soon, and as usual had radioed a few minutes before with their ETA and a journey update. The news was that, once again, poor Harry had been violently car-sick.

It was my first weekend at Highgrove, and even though I had Joan and Mrs Paddy, as Nesta was always called, to help me through, I was still feeling quite nervous. 'Oh dear, Your Royal Highness,' I said, fortunately remembering to use the correct greeting. 'I'll go and find one.' I looked outside and saw other cars pulling up in the back courtyard.

'I simply don't know what's wrong with the boy. He keeps on being ill whenever he goes on long car journeys,' added the Prince, pointing to a cupboard where he thought the buckets might be kept. 'At least this time it didn't happen in my car and all over my papers. It quite ruined the notes I was making for a speech.' He chuckled as he remembered the incident, then pointed through the window and said: 'Oh, here they are. Action stations.'

Quickly filling the bucket, I followed the Prince out to the red stretch limo containing Diana, the nanny and the boys. Dressed in black leggings and a jumper, Diana laughed as she handed Harry over to the nanny, Barbara Barnes. 'Do you mind taking him a moment, Barbara,' she giggled. 'I've got sick all over me.' A thoroughly fed-up Harry was deposited into Barbara's arms and rushed off to the nursery for a change of clothes.

Meanwhile William, now a large three-year-old, had jumped out of the other door and was running up to greet his father. The Prince scooped him up in his arms and whirled William, by now squealing with delight, around in the air.

'William, have you met Wendy yet?' asked Charles after a while. 'No, Papa,' he said as the Prince lowered him to the ground. Dressed in beige shorts and a blue jumper, William walked over to me and held out his hand. In a very grown-up voice he said: 'Hello, Windy [sic]. My name is William. How do you do?' I smiled as he turned his head back to Charles to make sure his father had seen him, before scampering off to the nursery.

Diana had gone into the house already and up to her room. Fay Marshalsea, the dresser on duty, had arrived earlier in the day, as had Charles's valet Ken Stronach, with my son James (as travelling butler) and the chef, Mervyn Wycherly, in two separate cars. The back courtyard was beginning to resemble a hotel car park. With no guests expected, I had been told it was going to be a quiet family weekend, despite the fact that more than ten staff, including policemen, were accompanying them.

That evening the Prince and Princess decided they would have their meal together on the card table in the sitting room. It was ordered for 8pm, and had been prepared by Mervyn earlier that day. The vegetables, nearly always picked from the Highgrove garden, were trimmed and left in cold salted water, ready to be microwaved at the last minute. And since they were having chicken, there was little left for him to do.

Mervyn, a muscular body-builder, who does evening work as a bouncer at a London nightclub to supplement his income, liked to do everything on a big scale. Not only is he twice the size of any other member of staff, he would also usually prepare double the amount of food needed. Shortly before 7pm all the travelling staff and I met for a quick gin in the first-floor staff sitting room overlooking the back garden. Then we sat down in our own private dining room on the ground floor to a selection of pizzas that would put most Italian restaurants to shame. Accompanying the pizzas were mountains of jacket potatoes, buckets of coleslaw and tubs of mayonnaise.

Our supper finished, it was time for Mervyn to start cooking Charles and Diana's meal. Since they had decided to eat as usual in the sitting room it would be taken in by James on a tray.

As they had their early evening bath, James laid the square card table with a white linen cloth, made sure that the fire was burning properly and emptied the wastepaper baskets.

Dressed in corduroys, shirt and sweater, Charles came down to the sitting room alone. James came back to the kitchen to tell Mervyn that Diana had decided not to have the chicken but would like just a salad instead. Mervyn shrugged his shoulders and muttered: 'Please herself. It sounds like it's going to be one of those weekends.'

Meanwhile James went to the large fridge and took out a small Schweppes bottle that had been filled with a gin martini cocktail. 'The Prince wants his martini now and dinner in twenty minutes. Is that all right, Merv?' he said before pouring the contents into a small crystal tumbler.

Twenty minutes later Diana popped her head around the kitchen door. 'I do hope I haven't put you out, Mervyn,' she said quietly. 'I just really didn't feel like the chicken this evening.' She looked subdued. 'That's quite all right, Ma'm,' lied Mervyn. 'I'll do you a nice salad.'

Then, turning to me, she said: 'I do hope everyone is looking after you, Wendy. It can all be a bit daunting at first, can't it?'

At 9.25pm Diana went upstairs to her room. Charles stayed reading in the sitting room until well past 11pm. But as soon as the Princess had gone up I went to the staff sitting room and had a quick drink with Barbara and the rest of the travelling staff. It was all quite surreal. Nobody gossiped openly about the Prince and Princess, although certain knowing looks were exchanged when they described the journey to Highgrove.

I was to start the next day at 7am, to tidy up the sitting room, clear out the fireplaces, clean the hallway and do the royal rooms as soon as the Prince and Princess were up. I was told that under no circumstances should I wake anyone up by making a noise, so I felt obliged to use a manual sweeper for the carpets.

Already in the kitchen were Mervyn and Ken, who, despite having been up drinking late into the night, still looked as fresh and clear-headed as the rest of us who had had a proper night's sleep.

By 7.20am I had done most of the downstairs dusting and laid the fires. I walked into the kitchen and found Ken by the kettle. 'Better get the Prince's Earl Grey tea,' he said, adding proudly, 'He always wants it dead on half past and I have never let him down.'

I waited downstairs as Ken went up to the Prince's room with a china cup and saucer on a tray.. Charles had quite a sweet tooth but tried to avoid sugar. Ken therefore always put a spoonful of honey into his tea.

At the same time Fay walked into Diana's adjoining bedroom and woke her up.

Within a few minutes there was a dreadful sound of grunting and moaning, followed by rhythmic thumping. Charles was doing his daily chin-ups on a bronze bar fixed above his bathroom door. In the months and years to come I could always tell when he was up, by the sound of the radio, usually Radio 4, and the bumping sound of his exercises.

Chin-ups were not the only thing the Prince did first thing in the morning, before his first bath of the day. Sometimes he went through a phase of sit-ups as well. For these he would get Ken, or Michael, his relief valet, to sit on his ankles on an exercise bed in the guest Blue Room as he struggled, in just a pair of white boxer shorts, to do his daily forty trunk curls.

Unfortunately I never witnessed the sight of Ken, somewhat embarrassed, dressed smartly in his blue blazer and flannels, sitting on Charles's feet as he put his body through its strenuous exercise routine!

Since it was November and quite chilly outside, Diana was unable to go for the early morning swim that was standard practice during the summer months. That first morning she took an early bath and came down, casually dressed, just before 8.30am. She found me cleaning the sitting-room carpet with the manual sweeper.

'Oh, Wendy, why on earth are you using that?' she said as she walked in. I explained that I didn't want to wake anyone up when I started at 7am. 'Well, why not leave all the hoovering until well after eight, and do the other things beforehand,' she said. 'The Prince and I certainly don't mind the noise as long as we are up. If you carry on using that old contraption it will take you hours to go over the whole house.'

With that she walked into the dining room, where a buffet of chopped fruits, cereals and linseed had been laid out on the side dresser the night before. The large mahogany table was covered for breakfast with a big plastic wipe-down tablecloth. Places were set at one end, the Prince at the head and Diana to his left, half a pink grapefruit and a couple of pots of yoghurt on her mat. At the far end of the table was a selection of the morning papers: *The Times* for the Prince, and the *Mail*, *Express* and her favourite new paper *Today* for the Princess. On Sundays Charles would take the *Sunday Times*, with Diana opting for the *Mail on Sunday* and *Sunday Express*.

. . .

Barbara Barnes usually prepared the boys' and her own breakfast from a tray that had been taken up the night before, allowing Charles and Diana to have the first few hours alone together. This did not always work, as William would sometimes toddle down to Diana's room and climb into bed with her after going for his early morning cuddle with Barbara in her bed.

Although Barbara, an attractive, slim woman with light brown hair, could be quite formal with the rest of the staff, she had a real bond with the boys, especially William. She was an old-fashioned nanny in the sense that her prime concern, although she would never admit it, was the heir to the throne. Although she didn't neglect Harry, you could see her very genuine affection and concern for the older son.

Shortly before 9am Charles and Diana moved into the sitting room with the papers and ordered another pot of coffee. I dashed upstairs with Fay to do the royal beds and bathrooms.

The Highgrove House rule was that staff could only enter royal rooms if the doors were left open. If shut it meant someone was inside and should not be disturbed. When it was windy this rule caused havoc, since one did not know if the rooms were occupied or whether the doors had been blown shut.

The linen in both Charles's and Diana's rooms was changed every time they stayed, which in the early days meant every weekend. If either was staying during the week, we changed the sheets every five days. The same rule applied to the Blue and Green guest bedrooms. The only time this did not hold was when the white sheets obviously needed to be changed; in Diana's case quite often, when they were caked in body make-up or full of crumbs and bits of chocolate from her or the boys nibbling things in bed.

On Diana's bedside table was a collection of photographs, of the children, her father Earl Spencer in weekend country clothes, and also her brother and sisters. A nearby chest was covered with little china ornaments. A portable weighing machine and a music centre were always unpacked by her dresser when she arrived and taken away at the end of the weekend.

I then went through to Diana's bathroom and cleaned out the large white bath, washing it down with a shower attachment she had recently had fitted. That morning she had obviously knocked one of the pictures lining the wall by the bath as she was getting out, so I rearranged that and put her Braun electric mouth jet spray back into its holder. The Princess always used this gadget morning and night. Similar to a machine used by a dentist, it fires a strong jet of water around the teeth and gums. She used Listerine, Charles a Floris Rose mouthwash.

She also kept her contraceptive pills in a mug by the sink. Diana took them religiously every day, even though there was never any sign that she and the Prince spent the night together.

Then, picking up one of the large bath towels from the floor and putting it back on its rail, I walked into Charles's room and repeated the procedure. On the Prince's dressing-table was a brown leather folder that opened out as a large photograph frame. Inside were pictures of William and Harry, Diana, and the Queen Mother.

A travelling alarm clock stood next to it, as well as a little writing pad on which he left notes to remind himself of things to check the following day. These could be domestic, as for example on that day, when he wrote in large block letters 'HUNT SUPPER – WHAT TIME?' On top of the pad was a battery-driven shaver. Little specks of beard were scattered over the table. He had obviously been shaving in bed that morning as he planned the day ahead. On the other side of his bed was a pile of hardback books, most of them barely opened.

Carefully removing Teddy, his threadbare companion everywhere he went, I remade the cot bed and plumped up the pillows. Teddy was laid on top of the bedspread.

In the bathroom Charles had his own set of linen hand towels, specially made for him by some nuns in America and with the Prince of Wales feathers crest blazoned across them. These, like Teddy, travelled everywhere with him. There were unfortunately only four of them, and, because they were linen, they would become creased after every use. It was my job to replace them each time – which some days meant dozens of times. Because of this I would be continually washing and ironing the wretched things – the whole chore made worse when one of them mysteriously disappeared!

On the sink was a tube of Maclean's toothpaste fitted into a small silver contraption that wound the tube from the bottom and made sure every last bit was squeezed out. When it came time for anything like toothpaste tubes or mouthwash bottles to be thrown away I had to inform the valet or dresser immediately so that they could replace the items.

After a quick hoover of both rooms I then went up to the nursery, to help Barbara with the boys' beds and to look over the carpet where William – nobody ever called him Wills – had spilt some Ribena. Barbara and I decided it was soon going to be time to change the cream-coloured carpet to something a bit more practical and hard-wearing.

· · ·

That first weekend was to set a pattern for many others during my first few years at Highgrove. The Prince and Princess visited most weekends, with or without guests, usually arriving on the Friday evening, with the Princess and the boys leaving on the Sunday after lunch. Charles usually stayed on Sunday nights and went straight to his engagements the following day.

When they were alone as a family, Saturdays were usually devoted to the boys. Charles might take them around the farm with him, or Diana might run them into Tetbury for a look at the shops. They were like any normal upper-class family, and both parents doted on the boys. It used to make all of us very angry that the Prince was always thought by the general public to be a remote and difficult father. William loved to put on old jeans and wellington boots and follow him around as he chatted to the gardeners deciding on what changes he was going to make.

Charles was keen to give his children a magical time in the country, and from the early days tried to encourage William in a love of horses. The Highgrove groom, Marion Cox, would lead him around the grounds on Smokey or Trigger, as Harry, still only fourteen months old, watched excitedly.

Diana, however, was less at ease at Highgrove. Soon after lunch that first Saturday, while Charles was outside with the boys in the garden, she appeared at the kitchen door.

'I've just come through for a cup of tea,' she said as she walked up to the kettle. 'Don't worry, I can do it myself.' On the tip of her nose hung a small drip of water, which she did not bother to wipe away. 'I've got a terrible cold,' she said weakly. 'And I really cannot face spending the whole day outside.'

As she waited for the kettle to boil she sat down on a kitchen chair and chatted. 'So what do you think then, Wendy?' she asked. 'Do you think you can be happy here? I've asked the Prince to have a look in at the Lodge a bit later on to see if there is anything that needs sorting out. Will it be OK to drop in about six?'

Then, after making herself a cup of tea, she got up and walked along the corridor to her sitting room. A few minutes later there was the sound of ballet music coming from her music centre. She spent the whole afternoon there, reading magazines, listening to music and making phone calls to friends, while Charles entertained the boys outside.

As the weather deteriorated and dusk fell the Prince, William and Harry, accompanied by Barbara, came back into the house. The fires, which had been lit in all the main rooms since before lunch, were now blazing and the boys went into Diana's sitting room to watch television. Charles went up to his room to change out of his muddy gardening clothes. He came down five minutes later and went into the sitting room.

The bell sounded again in the kitchen and James boiled the kettle. It was time for the Prince's afternoon cup of Earl Grey tea with a small glass of single malt Laphraoig whisky. Alongside the cup and saucer James placed a little glass-stoppered bottle full of the whisky, which Charles himself poured into the cup. There was probably only enough for a triple pub measure, but Charles always drank it – for health reasons, he would say, rather than because he needed something to calm his nerves!

Later that day, as I was sitting in the Lodge having a surreptitious cigarette, there was a knock at the door. The Prince, dressed in smart green trousers, a heavy jumper and wellingtons, was standing in the porch, Diana in a puffa jacket and jeans behind him.

'Hello, Wendy, I just wondered if you had everything you wanted,' said Charles kindly. As both of them stepped inside they removed their boots and walked around the house in their socks. Although it was perfectly natural, I suppose, it did seem funny later on that I had had the Prince and Princess of Wales padding around my house without any shoes on.

Charles walked slowly around the Lodge, occasionally nodding as Diana and I talked about what I wanted to do with my new home. Suddenly he stopped by the radiator in the sitting room. 'Is it damp in here, Wendy?' he asked with concern, as if it was one of life's great, serious questions. Then, getting down on his hands and knees, he tapped along the skirting board near the radiator. 'Damp!' he exclaimed. 'I knew it.'

After politely declining the offer of a drink, the Prince and Princess walked back to the porch. 'We must get back for another Mervyn special,' said Charles. 'We are both quite tired and want an early supper.' Both laughed as they walked arm in arm up the drive to the main house.

I remembered thinking how happy and contented they looked that evening. And how different it had been the night before, when Diana had obviously been crying. Maybe there was hope for them both. Maybe the tension that often surfaced between them was no more than a tiff, and they would both be genuinely all right together. At least I hoped so.

CHAPTER THREE

Happy Christmas

Small slices of roast lamb dropped to the floor as Diana hacked away at the joint on the kitchen sideboard. Larger, juicier pieces were expertly cut from the bone and quickly fingered into her mouth, as the Princess ravenously attacked the remnants of the staff lunch. 'This is great,' she declared between barely finished mouthfuls. 'I often think you lot have more interesting meals than we do.'

Lightly tanned, and dressed casually in a bright wool sweater and cords, Diana looked sensational. She and the Prince had returned from a tour of Australia several weeks earlier, but she was still on a high. It was Saturday evening and the Princess was talking about the film première of *Back to the Future* at London's Empire, Leicester Square, the previous Tuesday.

'It was such fun and so exciting,' she giggled, as a small piece of meat dropped to the floor. 'And there were *so* many photographers. I think they actually got some very good pictures of me. Did you see them all back here?' I went to one of the cupboards in the pantry and came back with a pile of newspapers packed with photographs of the occasion.

'Ooh, let me see them,' shouted Diana excitedly, letting the knife clatter on to the tiled floor. 'I don't think I've seen some of these yet.' Over numerous cups of tea, Diana, her detective Sergeant Barry Mannakee, Mervyn and I sat around the table poring over the pictures. Diana seemed to come alive – her eyes sparkled as she chatted away ten to the dozen about the film.

'*Noooo*,' she squealed at one stage. 'Barry, have you seen this one? It makes me look absolutely dreadful.' A picture of Diana in evening dress was taken from an unusual angle, making her shoulders look slightly hunched and her nose rather large. 'Why have they used this one?' she moaned. 'So many of the others were better. Why are they trying to make me look horrid?'

For nearly an hour we compared the pictures, flattering her on the good ones, and trying to convince her that the less complimentary shots were not quite as dreadful as she thought. It was beginning to be a bit boring.

'Are you sure, Wendy?' she pleaded, after I told her how one slightly gawky pose reminded me of a model I had seen in a recent edition of *Vogue*. 'You don't think it makes me look like a witch?' As she left the room I exchanged a glance with Mervyn.

Later that evening, after Diana had gone to her room, and as Charles surrounded himself with papers in his study, I went up to the staff sitting room to chat with Barry Mannakee. Barry was Diana's favourite detective, and everyone, including me, adored him. He was such a colourful and easy-going character. Tubby, gregarious and fun, he was an ideal personal protection officer for the Princess. He held a very privileged, though unspoken, position because he was so obviously favoured by Diana. She hung on to his every word, flirted with him outrageously, and pulled his leg in a way that suggested the two of them were very close.

There have been many rumours about them having an affair, but I am sure that is completely untrue. For Diana, Barry was simply a friend, someone she could rely on and trust. She had, after all, to entrust him with her life, and needed him as moral support on all her public engagements.

I had quickly come to realise that Diana needed constant reassurance and Barry was one of the few, along with her dresser, who could give it to her. One day, as they were leaving Highgrove for a job, Diana turned to him in the hall. Flashing a confident smile, since she obviously knew what his answer would be, she said, 'Barry, how do I look? Do you think these are the right earrings?' She pulled and smoothed down a skintight evening dress, and ran her fingers through her hair, which had been cut that morning. 'Do I look all right?' she repeated.

'Sensational, as you know you do,' laughed Barry as he walked towards the car door. 'I could quite fancy you myself.'

'But you do already, don't you?' quipped Diana coquettishly. 'Escort me to my car if you please.'

It was Barry, the son of working-class London parents, to whom Diana turned when she was unhappy or depressed. And it was Barry who would hug her when she was crying, and give her the reassurance she needed. He was discreet and never boasted or talked about how close he was to the Princess. But his relationship with her upset other officers, especially Colin Trimming, the Prince's PPO (personal protection officer), who considered he was overstepping the mark.

Barry was later to confide to me that Trimming had warned him about being 'overfriendly' with the Princess and told him 'to cool it'. 'What can I do about it?' he asked me, sweeping his hand though his thinning light brown hair. 'I mean, it's ridiculous for anyone to even think I am more than her detective.' He went on to describe the time Diana broke down in tears a few hours before a recent public engagement. 'She kept on saying she couldn't go ahead with it, and just collapsed into my arms,' he said. 'I hugged her and stopped her crying. What else would you have done?'

Whether the Prince was jealous or whether he was concerned about how friendly his wife was becoming with her detective I will never know. But all the police officers had to report to Colin, letting him know about anything that had happened when they were on duty with Diana. And every time she tapped Barry's arm, or said affectionately, 'What would I do without you?' it was noted down and reported. In the end her light, cheerful gestures were totally misinterpreted and led to Barry's downfall, and he was moved away to different duties. Two years later he was killed in a freak road accident.

Colin Trimming was and is a very reliable detective, and the Prince holds him in extremely high regard. It was he who accompanied Charles on his visits to Camilla in the early days. There is a level of trust between them that could never be doubted or broken. Diana used to find his power quite intimidating, since she knew that everything she did was being watched and scrutinised. Wherever she went, whomever she spoke to, she knew that everything would be reported back to

'Trimming' as she called him, and passed on to Charles. 'It's like living in a nightmarish police state,' she would often say to me – only half-joking.

Before going home to the Lodge that evening I went into the hall to check if all the lights were off. There was a note on the hall table from the Prince to his valet Michael Fawcett. On specially embossed Prince of Wales notepaper he had scrawled, 'Please make sure all the lights are off. We need a bulb for the right-hand picture light on the mantelpiece in the hall – the one pointing at the picture with P of W feathers on the frame.' It was signed with a large C. For a man with such a busy schedule and royal duties coming out of his ears it was amusing to think he still bothered about the lights being left on at night.

. . .

That December morning started like most Sundays, with me cleaning out all the fireplaces and shouting at Paddy for more wood. 'Don't put so much on the bloody things,' he would grumble as I asked for yet more logs. 'It's like a ruddy Turkish bath in some rooms as it is.'

I had finally been sent the standard Buckingham Palace Guide to Royal Housekeeping the day before, and was mentally ticking off the chores as I went through them. The guide's instructions are very clear.

HOUSEKEEPING IN ROYAL HOUSES

DAYS WHEN THE HOUSE IS EMPTY.
Hand vacuum all soft furnishings, pelmets, window seats/curtains etc. Clean mirrors and pictures and glass tops. Wipe woodwork, vacuum carpets and dust. Clean staff bedrooms and staff areas, change sheets and catch up on all other household laundry.

BEFORE ANYONE ARRIVES.
Arrange flowers and plants, put out towels, open windows and draw blinds.

WHEN A MEMBER OR MEMBERS OF THE FAMILY ARE IN.
7am. Thoroughly dust all downstairs areas and carpet-sweep where necessary. Straighten magazines, empty wastepaper baskets, plump cushions, draw curtains. Set staff table for breakfast (and clear away afterwards).

Whilst TRHs [Their Royal Highnesses] are at breakfast – tidy bedrooms and make beds, clean bathrooms and change towels (may only be enough time to do this roughly and return to do a thorough job later). Check water in flowers/plants. Start on nursery – beds, bathrooms, change towels, dust and vacuum and check flowers.

Set staff table for lunch and clear up after staff lunch. Whilst TRHs at lunch check bathrooms, study, sitting room.

Off.

6pm. Check all downstairs rooms, guest bathrooms, HRH study, sitting room, bedrooms and bathrooms (empty waste baskets, plump pillows, straighten magazines, wipe basins, straighten towels).

Set staff dinner table – clear away afterwards.

Whilst TRHs are bathing, re-do study, sitting room and turn down beds. Do bathrooms (basins, baths, toilets, etc and replace towels when needed).

Close windows and put on lamps and draw curtains (when necessary).

GENERAL RULES.
Whenever there is a workman or outsider in the house – whoever it is, there should be a member of staff in attendance, and any personal items and photographs should be covered up.

· · ·

William and Harry had breakfast in the nursery with Barbara, while Charles and Diana came down to the dining room. You could have cut the atmosphere with a knife. As the coffee pot was taken through we all heard Diana shriek: 'Oh for God's sake, Charles!' and then the sound of a banging door and footsteps running up to her bedroom. It was, unfortunately, going to be one of those days.

I was already upstairs doing the bathrooms, but had fortunately made a start on the Prince's room and not Diana's. I was carefully placing his Teddy back on top of the rust-red bedspread as I heard her rush into her room and fling herself down on to her double bed. She was crying uncontrollably and I felt trapped in a terrible dilemma. All my natural instincts told me to go next door and comfort her. But it would have been totally inappropriate, misconstrued as 'overstepping the mark'. In the case of one footman who was exceptionally close to the Princess and who did comfort her at times like this, it led to his being moved to other duties. And the Princess's crying fits and moods were at times no worse than those experienced by many parents coming to terms with a daughter's difficult adolescence.

I looked at the Prince's Teddy – an ancient, patched-up cuddly toy that was packed by his valet in a plastic shirt-bag and accompanied the Prince everywhere. I could see a bit of stuffing starting to peep through Teddy's left arm, and made a mental note to send him back to Charles's nanny Mabel Anderson, the only woman allowed to do repairs, who would cover the area with a small patch of chamois leather.

Looking at Teddy, knowing that he would be chauffeur-driven for his repairs, and hearing the sounds of sobbing coming from Diana's room, I felt caught up in some dreadful, surreal tragedy.

As I walked down the back staff stairs I could hear Barbara leading William and Harry, who was still in nappies, down to the dining room. William ran straight to his father, shouting, 'Papa!' The Prince, who had stayed by himself in the dining room for nearly an hour after Diana's outburst, rushed towards his son, scooping him up in his arms. Diana's papers – the *Mail on Sunday* and *Sunday Express* – were left untouched on the table.

With an hour to go before I had to set the staff table for lunch, I went along to have a chat with Fay Marshalsea, the dresser, in her room. Fay was slaving over an ironing board. On her bed were several outfits that the Princess would be wearing later that afternoon. Happy-go-lucky Fay, whose principal ambition at that time was to meet a suitable man and get married, was having a moan about being at Highgrove and all the ironing she had to do.

'You know, I sometimes wonder why I ever took this job at all,' she said as she carefully took the creases out of a heavy skirt. 'I know it sounds glamorous and all that at first, but really all we are here for is to skivvy around after some very spoiled people who, if they are not crying their eyes out, are ridiculously demanding. It's not as if we are paid very much, is it?'

I made no reply, hearing a noise outside the room. I put my finger to my lips to tell Fay to keep quiet as I looked out. I just caught sight of Diana, barefoot, tiptoeing down the staff corridor. She had obviously been hovering around outside and had heard the tail-end of Fay's complaints. 'Oh, God,' muttered Fay, after she had gone away. 'That really has torn it.'

I was rapidly beginning to understand that royal service was just as precarious for the staff as for the family itself. While the royals could complain about the whispers and lack of privacy they endured through living in a large household, the staff too had to live under similar conditions. Diana, an arch spy, was expert at creeping about barefoot and hearing comments made about her behind her back. She had obviously heard everything, because within a few minutes the phone in Fay's room rang. Fay was to go to the Princess's room AT ONCE.

Later that day she recounted the terrible dressing-down she had received. She walked through the heavy fire door and into Diana's pink-and-white-papered room to find the Princess staring out of the window overlooking the back of the house. Speaking slowly at first, Diana said in a controlled, flat voice, 'Do you quite realise, Fay, how lucky you are to be here? It costs us a great deal to look after you all, you know. We feed you and house you. Where do you think you would be without us?'

Warming to the argument, she continued in a slightly louder tone, 'How DARE you complain about things when you have literally everything done for you.' She didn't seem to care that she had heard Fay complaining by subterfuge. She wanted Fay to apologise for what she had said, and to sound genuine about it. The Princess was at her most effectively brutal that day, and when I saw Fay later on she looked quite shaken by the confrontation.

The Princess did, however, have a point of sorts. Although the pay was appalling, considering the hours we worked and the discretion required as members of the Royal Household, staff were allowed many perks and discounts not available to the general public. In those days most of us had grace and favour houses, with the Duchy paying all bills. If anything went wrong we could call in plumbers and electricians at any time of the day or night and send the bills to the household. All food was effectively free, since when the royal chefs were on duty they had to cook for us as well as the Prince and Princess. Another source of great delight for the staff was the discount available from well-known stores and manufacturers, sometimes amounting to eighty per cent.

Naturally, the same discounts applied to the royal family. Charles might seem set in his ways about lots of things, but when it came to soaps and lotions he could be quite adventurous, and made full use of the manufacturers' generosity. He would ask his valet to lay out various types and brands on the bed in the Blue Room to try, and for a while was keen on Floris's Rose Geranium blend, which we all thought quite racy for him! Every bath had a big block of this translucent soap, but one day Charles had a violent change of heart about the smell and ordered it all to be thrown out. Nobody quite seemed to know what had changed his mind.

On top of this were all the free gifts sent by the lorry-load to the couple either at Kensington Palace or at Highgrove. When that happened there was a general free-for-all after the Prince and Princess had had first choice. The rest was burnt in big incinerators at the back of the house. It never ceased to amaze me how many gifts and clothes were thrown away. Even after the first few months at Highgrove it would make me feel quite sick with anger at such waste. The clothes and ornaments were systematically put into black plastic bin-liners every month and stuffed by Paddy or his workmen into the incinerator. When I asked Fay once whether anyone would notice if we took just one beautiful blouse, she replied: 'It's more than my job's worth. I am told we have to burn the stuff rather than let it fall into the hands of someone who would try and sell it for its royal associations.' Fay looked quite upset as she watched hundreds of pounds' worth of clothes go up in smoke.

It was just a few weeks away from Christmas and two trees had been ordered from the local arboretum in Tetbury – free of course for the Prince and Princess. For people who had so much money I was beginning to understand how they retained it – they *never* seemed to pay for anything!

Paddy and Fred from the estate came in with the trees. One, the larger one, was to go in the hall; the other in the nursery on the top floor. When I came to unpack the boxes of decorations from the cellar I was quite surprised at how naff and ordinary they were. There were multi-coloured little animals, star shapes, fairies and lots of glittering cheap stuff. We attached baubles as well, but the finished tree in the hall was not, quite honestly, what I would have expected. It did not seem to be a priority to make everything look magical and wonderful downstairs – that was reserved for the boys in the nursery.

A week before the Highgrove staff party on Sunday, December 15, we were all given £20 to buy ourselves a Christmas present. I remember thinking how odd it was to go out and choose one's own present – it might have been better to have been given a cash Christmas bonus, along with a token present chosen by the Boss. However, I went into Tetbury and bought myself a Parker pen, which I then carefully wrapped and handed over to the butler.

Shortly before noon that day we all lined up in the green and red dining room, which stank of diesel fumes because the flue was near the boiler. Charles, Diana, William and Harry walked down the line, joking and chatting with us as they handed over the gifts. Both Charles and Diana threw themselves into the occasion. They seemed genuinely happy to be surrounded by all their staff, from butlers down to temporary gardeners, handing out presents and wishing everyone a happy Christmas.

Then it was on to the hall for drinks, followed by lunch prepared and served by J. Lyons and Co. The whole operation was executed with military precision by Colonel Creasy of the Prince of Wales's office. Kitchen work-tops had to be cleared that morning by 9am precisely, and all equipment removed, so that there were no 'misunderstandings' over cutlery and plates later on.

Wine was served freely and by the end of a splendid meal most people were swapping intimate stories and generally letting their hair down. William and Harry had gone up to the nursery, but Charles and Diana circulated from table to table. Both wore funny hats, and laughed and joked as if they didn't have a care in the world. It made quite a change from the usual household dramas!

After coffee, Charles made a speech. He apologised for his somewhat eccentric ways, cracked a joke at several people's expense and then finished by saying: 'As you all know, Diana and I are terribly proud of everything you do for us. We literally could not manage if you were not around. All of you must remember that you are our ambassadors; what you do, and how you behave, reflects directly on us. Thank you and Merry Christmas.'

As everyone applauded Paddy turned to me and squeezed my thigh. 'D'you think you'll stay, then?' he said with a wink. 'It's not so bad, is it?'

1986

CHAPTER FOUR

Sarah and Andrew

Bright early morning sunlight broke through the small panes of glass in Diana's bedroom as Evelyn Dagley, the Princess's dresser, and I changed the royal sheets. Although a January frost had sealed a hard layer of silver over the garden and trees outside, Diana's simply decorated room was sweltering as a result of Highgrove's cantankerous central heating being turned up to its maximum level.

I ran my hands over the bottom sheet to smooth it out and stopped. My fingers closed over two pieces of pink wax, pinched into the shape of two ugly, fluorescent slugs. I looked up into Evelyn's elfin face and dark eyes. She shrieked with laughter. 'They must have been together last night, if only for a while,' she snorted. 'And those things in your hand are the Princess's earplugs. She has to wear them every time she shares a bed with the Prince because of his snoring.'

The discovery of the earplugs made me chuckle. I couldn't help wondering if she put them in straight away in front of Charles, or waited until he temporarily dozed off by her side. Evidently Ev mentioned something to the Princess, because later that day she came across me in the staff corridor and stopped for a chat.

'I hear you found my plugs very amusing this morning, Wendy,' she giggled. 'The thing is I cannot stand his snoring. And rather than try and sleep with fingers in my ears or a pillow wrapped around my head I picked up this idea from long-distance flights. Not bad for ingenuity, don't you think?'

I watched her half skip, half jog down to the brushing room to pick up some wellington boots for outside. It all seemed so funny and light-hearted at the time, but the snoring was later to become a pretext for their not sharing a bed, as with so many married couples. It led to a permanent regime of separate bedrooms. The Princess would say she wanted to go to bed early, and didn't want to be disturbed by her husband as he came up hours later.

I used to think that it was perhaps at this stage of their marriage, in 1986, that they missed the opportunity of some sort of long-term reconciliation. If only they had made more of an effort to get things working then, the marriage might have turned out all right after all. For in 1986 Diana was still making an effort to be loving and affectionate to her husband. Occasionally she would run up to him outside in the garden and fling her arms around him. The trouble was that he rarely reciprocated the affection she craved at the time she needed it.

On some days he seemed almost embarrassed by such a display of affection, and would half-heartedly return her advances in a lukewarm fashion as if he had other things on his mind. When that happened Diana would be plunged into despair, and would run into the house and the sanctuary of her sitting room. Charles would be left standing outside in his muddy cords and wellingtons with a bemused William and Harry, shouting after her, 'Darling, come back. Of course I want to hug you.'

On other days it would be Charles who crept up on Diana, grabbing her from behind and trying to kiss her playfully on the neck. Then it would be Diana's turn to spurn the advances, pulling herself away from him, and muttering something along the lines of 'Not here. Everyone can see us.' Any staff in the vicinity would scamper away to engross themselves in duties they had suddenly remembered, for fear of witnessing another spectacular display of marital fireworks.

. . .

The sound of laughter filled the hall as the throaty, upper-crust voice of a Sloaney female shouted out, 'Cooee. Is anyone there?' It was Saturday afternoon on January 25 and Sarah Ferguson had just arrived.

'Well, where is he?' bellowed Fergie.

'Who?' smirked Diana. 'Charles or Andrew?'

'Not Andrew, silly,' replied Sarah. 'Charlie-boy, your hubby.'

'Oh, he's not here. You must have known that, Sarah. I told you that last weekend. It's just you, me, Andrew and the boys. I don't even have Barbara on this weekend.'

'Where's the drinks cabinet, then,' joked Sarah, and both dissolved into a fit of giggles that any pair of fourteen-year-old schoolgirls would be proud of.

Since there was no nanny on, I said I would assist Evelyn with her work, as she might be called on by Diana to help out with William and Harry. I walked up to greet Sarah Ferguson in the hall, taking her slightly tatty, battered old suitcase up to the Green Room where she would be staying. I unzipped the case and laid Fergie's clothes out on the bed: a pair of old jeans, a thick tweed skirt, and several nondescript blouses. It had all been packed in a hurry and was crumpled, and some of it didn't look particularly clean either. Fortunately Ev arrived at this point and I left her to sort out the clothes that needed pressing. 'Just look at this stuff, will you,' she tutted as she went through the piles of grey-white underwear. 'God help us all.'

On the way down the back stairs I could hear that Prince Andrew had just arrived. Dressed in heavy corduroy trousers, a checked shirt and dark yellow sweater, he greeted Diana extremely affectionately with a kiss on either cheek. He then made a bellowing noise and gave Sarah a bear-hug, kissing her full on the lips. 'I can see who is the more popular one here,' laughed Diana.

William and Harry loved seeing their uncle, and Andrew knew this. It allowed him, quite shamelessly, to play the buffoon in front of them, entertaining both excited children with numerous practical jokes. He had them in fits by firing a water pistol at Sarah and Diana as they walked around the back garden. Later on, as Diana was preparing to take them up to bed, he kept them entertained with strange farting noises, pulling grotesque expressions that William in particular thought hilarious.

While Sarah was a simple, relatively uncomplicated girl at this time I had heard horror stories about Andrew from my son and other staff at Buckingham Palace. As a royal child he had been brought up, like Charles, to be waited on hand and foot, and as a result tended to barge his way around the house, expecting to be looked after and served for every whim. It was explained to me that it wasn't his fault, simply that he had been reared in a system that allowed him practically anything he wanted.

There was a childishness to his character that sat somewhat uneasily with the physique of a sturdy twenty-six-year-old man. James told me, 'Prince Andrew was like his father the Duke of Edinburgh, and unmistakably the Queen's favourite son. There was an inherited bluffness and directness which could be off-putting, until you realised it was usually just a front for getting through otherwise awkward situations. Unlike Edward, Andrew was the archetypal man's man, whose sense of humour perfectly matched the Windsors' delight in crude, coarse, lavatorial jokes. Whoopee cushions were constantly hidden under guests' chairs – jokes about farts the stock in trade of his conversational banter.'

James added that, unlike Edward, who was unusually shy and private about getting dressed and undressed in front of staff, Andrew took delight in strutting around his apartment with nothing on, barking instructions as staff hurriedly picked up wet towels and dirty clothes strewn around the bed.

One occasion James remembers vividly was when he went with Andrew and his detective for a weekend's shooting on the Duke of Westminster's estate. The Prince had just gone off for a bath when the bell rang. 'Come in, come in,' shouted Andrew as James knocked on the door. 'Where the bloody hell are my black socks – the ones with the stripe at the top?' He was standing in the middle of the room stark naked, vigorously rubbing his wet hair with a towel, another two tossed into the corner by the dressing-table. James looked down, then up – the talk about Andrew's legendary libido and stamina had undoubtedly been exaggerated.

Staff were practically invisible as far as he was concerned, since they were there to serve and not to question his actions. As a result he was not the most popular man to work for at Buckingham Palace. In particular it was his thoughtlessness that upset most of the housemaids and valets who worked under him. Apparently his bedtime habits as a single man left a lot to be desired, and a collection of scrunched-up, soiled tissues usually lay scattered around the bed each morning for staff to collect after they had made his bed.

There was a good example of his offhand manner that evening, as Diana and Sarah were reading the boys their bedtime story. A telephone call intended for the pantry was somehow misdirected through to the drawing room where Andrew was flicking through some magazines. Frances Simpson, the Kensington Palace housekeeper, was on the line and didn't recognise his voice. When she asked for me, Andrew apparently replied, 'Wrong bloody room, idiot,' before hanging up.

Andrew was the antithesis of Edward, who whenever he came to Highgrove, either alone or with a girlfriend, was utterly charming and polite. Where Andrew would barge in front of you through a doorway, Edward would stop, step to one side and let you through, whoever you were.

That evening, with William and Harry safely tucked up in bed in the nursery, Andrew, Diana and Sarah had dinner on card tables in the sitting room. As we all traipsed up to the staff sitting room after supper we could hear the sound of laughter. It was the first time we had heard real happiness in that room for some time.

The following morning suggested that the night before had been particularly riotous in the guest bedrooms. By all the evidence Andrew and Sarah had decided to try out both rooms in the space of a few hours. As I replaced the voluminous linen sheets on the king-sized beds I felt quite entitled to a little moan. Having Sarah and Andrew to stay was going to mean a lot of work. Several staff at Buckingham Palace had warned me that I would be changing both beds every day for the length of their visit.

At Highgrove without her husband, Diana seemed to flourish as never before. She suddenly took much more interest in the gardens and grounds, accompanying the boys and Andrew and Sarah outside in the cold where normally she would have chosen to stay indoors.

William was by now able to sit quite comfortably on his pony Smokey, with the help of the groom, Marion Cox, and loved being able to show off his riding skills to the grown-ups. Diana had decked the boys out in trendy jeans and sweaters, and the whole group had races in the garden until lunch, which they ate in the dining room. This was a treat for the boys as well, since normally they had their food upstairs with Nanny in the nursery. That afternoon it rained and children and adults mingled freely around the house. Everyone was in and out of each other's rooms, like some large extended family.

Seeing Diana at Highgrove with people of her own generation, it suddenly struck me that it could be the happy, family home that Charles intended when he first moved in. The trouble was that it only seemed relaxed when either he or Diana wasn't there. Put them together and the problems resurfaced all over again.

The Monday morning before they left Sarah popped her head around the kitchen door and asked for some more writing paper for her room. I was struck by how pleasant but ordinary she was in the flesh, without any proper make-up on. Dressed in a long skirt and jumper, and with her hair tied into a ponytail, she looked more like a prep school matron than a Duchess in waiting. 'I've just got to send some letters though – on Highgrove paper,' she giggled. 'I promised a friend, who will be so *terribly* impressed.'

If only Sarah Ferguson had stayed like that, an excitable, unpretentious upper-class girl. Marriage brought her attention and a list of privileges that she could never have dreamed of. It was quite to turn her head.

That Monday Diana was picked up by the red royal helicopter at 2.30pm. As she walked up the steps she turned and waved to the staff who stood in the hallway to see her off. She looked happy and content, in control of her own life and at ease with Charles safely out of the picture.

· · ·

The change was remarkable the following weekend when Charles and Diana were back together at Highgrove. A cold, hard wind blew outside, but it was nothing compared to the chill within. There was none of the relaxed atmosphere of the weekend before and Diana looked on the verge of tears for much of the time.

Like most of the staff, I tried very hard not to take sides or form judgements about what was going on between them as they stormed and argued around the house. I suppose that I just wanted them to kiss and make up, and make our lives easier as well as theirs. But it was on that early February weekend that I began to see the absolute desperation and frustration felt by both the Prince and the Princess, having to live within a marriage that was patently falling apart at the seams.

The Prince's indifference would have been crushing for anyone. One afternoon as the boys were playing upstairs with Barbara, Diana raced out after her husband as he marched through the back door to look at his Aston Martin in the garage. As he strode over the slippery wooden coal-hole cover Diana followed close behind, slipped and ended up on her bottom. Charles carried on walking, and didn't even bother to look behind him as Diana sat whimpering in the drizzle.

Paddy later laughed about Diana going 'arse over tit' on the board, but I found the whole scene extremely upsetting. The Prince seemed to have grown so indifferent to his wife, so aloof and uncaring, that I realised then that a long-term reconciliation was unlikely.

However difficult and devious she might be, and however much she might have been to blame for their marriage problems, my heart bled for Diana. Nevertheless, despite the hurt and the anger, the royal show had to continue, as much for the sake of the children as for Queen and country.

. . .

The bond and closeness between Barbara and the boys meant there were no tantrums or scenes while their parents were away skiing. Everything followed a set routine, and they would be woken and dressed at the same time every morning. Occasionally William would refuse to wear his gloves or raincoat, and would then be told in no uncertain terms by Barbara that he wouldn't be going out at all that day unless he did.

All the staff were told by Diana and Charles to tell the boys off if they were rude or naughty. But it was only allowed to be a verbal ticking-off. Diana was vehemently against slapping the children, and only rarely did it herself. If she heard that someone else had done it, she would have hit the roof.

The most important time for the boys when their parents were away was just after 6.30pm when they were getting ready for bed. Clad in green and white striped pyjamas and clutching their teddy bears, they would wait expectantly for a call from their mother and father. Diana hated leaving them behind, and Barbara was required to give a highly detailed account of everything they had been up to during the day before she hung up.

Barbara was used to and enjoyed being the formal royal nanny, and found it difficult to understand why Diana wanted to take such an active part in her children's upbringing, when so many other royals had handed over most responsibility to their nannies. Since the end of October 1985 William had attended a £200-a-term private nursery in Notting Hill, West London, which was taming him a little, but Barbara still felt it necessary to make him conform to what she thought was the proper dress and behaviour of a young boy who would one day be King.

'He needs to be treated differently because he is different,' Barbara would often say. 'It's no good Diana pretending he can have a completely normal life, because he can't.' It was already possible to see the seeds of discontent growing between Diana and Barbara. Eventually this would turn into a power battle, which Diana would win.

Barbara would listen patiently as Diana explained she wanted the boys dressed in the clothes *she* had chosen, and not kitted out in old-fashioned, boring gear that made them look as if they were of a different era. And she would grumble quietly about the state of their shoes and the holes in their favourite trousers as she took control after the boys had spent a weekend alone with their mother. 'We'd better be having you out of these things, hadn't we, William?' she would say as Diana pulled away for an official engagement. 'They will be falling off you soon unless we change.' William and Harry addressed her as 'Baba', and even though she could sometimes be very strict with them, both boys adored her.

. . .

No sooner were the Prince and Princess back from their skiing trip than Charles flew off to Texas. Before he left on February 17, he walked around the house with me, pointing out the areas he wished me to discuss with the interior designer Dudley Poplak, who had decorated much of the house in the early days. By the end of our half-hour visit I had two sheets of paper covered with instructions.

'Oh, and by the way, I've arranged to send you on a flower-arranging course in London. Now, you mustn't take offence,' he added, 'because I know you do them very nicely in your own particular way. I just thought it might be a good idea for you to learn a few different new arrangements with the professionals.'

Such attention to detail was typical of the Prince. As he left I thought there couldn't be many men who would have considered sending their housekeeper to London for a flower-arranging course, let alone the Prince of Wales!

Charles seemed more alive and enthusiastic than I had ever seen him before as we walked around discussing Highgrove.

'The Prince looks happy,' I said to one of the policemen as I walked down to the Lodge after he had left for America. 'I wonder why,' he replied with a knowing grin. 'He must be in love,' I said absent-mindedly. 'Perhaps,' he answered. 'But with whom?'

CHAPTER FIVE

Hard Hats

It had now been five months since I had joined the staff at High-grove, and Paddy was beginning to warm to me. His poor wife Nesta was seriously ill with cancer, but Paddy still came in every day, and nothing was ever really decided without his permission. Dear Paddy, who still smelt strongly of horses, who still had the Irish gift of the gab, would constantly follow me around the house.

'You should have seen this place in the old days,' he would say. 'Before the Princess got her claws into it. We all had a grand old time. It's the Prince's home, you see, and he feels comfortable here. That's why she mustn't be allowed to spoil things for him.'

Blunt-speaking but roguishly charming, Paddy had seen so much of the Prince with all his other friends that he felt Diana to be an outsider. He was at Highgrove in the early 'camping days', as Charles described them, when Diana, accompanied by Andrew and Nicholas Soames, had stayed in October 1980. The fact that Diana stayed another day with the Prince alone was not generally known, but Paddy had been there and had been party to the illicit weekend.

His loyalty to the Prince knew no bounds, and Charles was aware of that. The two would chat for hours when out hunting, Charles riding and Paddy acting as his groom. And it is Paddy who knows the real secrets about Charles and the Royal Family, more than any living Household servant. He also had a sixth sense where security was concerned, once becoming aware of intruders in the grounds by intuition before the alarms started to ring.

Although the security arrangements at Highgrove were strict, there was always the possibility of a random attack. Safety precautions were quite elaborate; they included a special secure room designed to cope with such an event, the location of which was not apparent to the casual observer.

.　　.　　.

Despite the gradual disintegration of their marriage, Charles and Diana still tried to spend as many weekends as possible with the children at Highgrove. To cope with the obvious friction between them, and for security reasons, the Prince would arrive in a separate car, followed by Diana with the nursery. Increasingly, however, Charles would arrive the day before Diana and leave the day after she went back to London on the Sunday afternoon. Diana, her weight and moods fluctuating by the week, would arrive looking drained. With her head bowed she would ask where the Prince was on some occasions, and on others not bother.

The only consistent fact about their weekends together now was that Diana would nearly always leave in tears. Rushing out of the back door, she was often unable even to mouth a goodbye because she was crying so much. The children, accompanied by Barbara Barnes, would follow, bewildered by all the commotion.

Usually Charles would race down a few seconds later, and give Diana a peck on the cheek in front of everyone, saying, 'Goodbye, darling. I do hope you feel better tomorrow,' or something equally unconvincing. Diana, her eyes still puffy and red from crying, would look away and say 'Bye' before getting into the car with Harry on her lap.

And so the weekends took on a familiar pattern. Yet underneath the terrible drama playing out before us we, the staff, had to maintain appearances and keep a large house and estate running smoothly. 'The sooner he gets rid of that one, the better,' said Paddy one afternoon over a cup of tea in the kitchen. Everyone knew he was talking about Diana, but nobody picked him up on the conversation.

.　　.　　.

As each new member of staff came to Highgrove, he or she was introduced and made welcome by 'old hands' in the bar. There was usually a strict code of silence when it came to royal gossip, at least until everyone felt absolutely sure of the new face. Even then, we were usually

THE HOUSEKEEPER'S DIARY

very wary. The royals inspire the utmost loyalty in their staff, and up until Diana's tacit acceptance of her friends' talking to Andrew Morton, most of us maintained that loyalty.

Even though we knew about the rows, the tears and the heartache we were happy to follow the accepted line whenever we were asked if all the stories in the papers were true. Standard answer Number One to people who had just joined was 'No, I think they are fine really.' This might be followed by 'Well, every couple has its ups and downs.'

As spring moved towards early summer, Charles and Diana spent increasing amounts of time travelling apart, but returning to Highgrove for weekends with the boys. They were together for the weekend before the Queen's sixtieth birthday on April 21.

It was a time of high drama for young Prince William. Just a few months short of his fourth birthday, he was due to attend the thanksgiving service at Windsor and ride back in the carriage with the Queen. Barbara had told him how important an event it was going to be, and William, suddenly taking the matter extremely seriously, rose to the occasion. He wanted to know over and over again exactly who was going to be there, and what he was expected to do. He loved the attention the whole matter was bringing him.

Diana, excited to see her son so caught up in the celebrations, arranged for her hairdresser to travel to Highgrove to trim his hair the day beforehand, and William was thrilled to be going through the same rigmarole and preparation as his mother.

Later that day, after they had all departed for Windsor, I watched the coverage of the service on television in the Lodge. Within a minute of my switching it off the phone was ringing.

'Wendy, thank God you're there.' It was Ken Stronach, the Prince's valet, ringing from Windsor Castle. 'I've tried every extension in the house, and there was no reply. Listen, you have got to help with something extremely important.' Barely able to speak through panic, he added: 'The Prince has left the Queen's birthday present on the desk in his study. You will see a small box of chocolates wrapped in gold paper. He wants them brought over to Windsor immediately, and since all the drivers appear to be tied up, and I am rushed off my feet here, I want you please to bring them.'

I looked at my old Nissan car outside the Lodge, and thought of the ninety-mile trip to Windsor from Highgrove. I asked Ken why someone couldn't simply pop out and buy another box of chocolates,

44

rather than go the expense of getting me to drive down there. 'They have to be those chocolates,' explained Ken. 'He says they are special ones.'

Reluctantly I agreed to do the drive, but thought the whole incident a typical waste of time and money. The Prince was forever getting staff to drive halfway round the country to collect things he either wanted or had forgotten. Sometimes he even sent a chauffeur to pick up vegetables. I don't think Charles even thought about the expense or the sheer wastefulness of his demands, in the same way that he didn't realise the hypocrisy of making speeches about fuel conservation one day, and driving in a ten-mile-to-the-gallon Bentley another.

. . .

Shortly before their official visit to Canada and Japan, the Prince and Princess spent a night at the house. The tension between them had reached breaking point, and was to augur badly for the tour that lay ahead. Arriving late at night, Diana had gone straight to bed and refused to eat with Charles in the sitting room. And the following morning, as she returned from her early morning swim, she stomped through the terrace door and upstairs in a foul temper, brow furrowed and eyes blazing. In the corridor by her room she bumped into the Prince, but as he tried to speak to her, Diana ran into the bedroom and slammed the door in his face.

'Diana, don't treat me like that,' said Charles in a perplexed tone of voice. 'What on earth is the matter with you?'

'Just leave me alone, will you,' screeched Diana from behind the door. Neither spoke to the other throughout the day.

Downstairs in the kitchen and pantry, we felt on tenterhooks. The atmosphere was terrible, since we knew scenes like these led to some very hostile treatment of staff.

In times of crisis Charles and Diana reacted in very different ways. Charles, who could be extremely volatile in the short term, usually became more formal and reserved when in the middle of some row with his wife. Even if Diana had just slapped him or called him a 'pathetic old fart' he would still try to retain his dignity in the face of adversity.

The Princess, however, might go into a terrible sulk for days after a scene, refusing to communicate with anybody apart from the most grudging of monosyllables. Her other reaction was tears and shouting at staff – something that poor Evelyn, her dresser, knew better than most.

. . .

In the summer months up to and beyond Prince Andrew's wedding to Sarah Ferguson, the house continued to be used for family weekends. As the weather improved Diana seemed to find her time at Highgrove more bearable, even if the quieter mood appeared to be more of an uneasy truce than a solid reconciliation between herself and Charles.

The Princess would usually have her swim before breakfast, doing length after length for about ten minutes, and then returning to her room for a bath. Charles would usually wait until the afternoon for his swim, and then encourage the boys to go in with him. In all my years at Highgrove, I can barely remember a time when Charles and Diana swam together.

Special friends came and went, in particular the MP Nicholas Soames and his wife, Hugh and Emilie Van Cutsem, and ex-King Constantine of Greece with his wife Queen Anne-Marie and mother the Queen of Denmark. Sometimes Lord and Lady King would be invited for the weekend, and they in turn became very friendly with King Constantine. Then aged forty-six, Constantine was every inch what you might have expected from a foreign king, who ran his family and household on very traditional lines.

In the weeks up to the family holiday in Balmoral Dudley Poplak came to make another inspection of the house. We walked around the rooms, chatting, and discussing the state of the carpets, paintwork and upholstery.

Dudley, a large, slightly tubby man, had a wonderful effect on the Princess, who adored his sense of humour and knowledge about spiritual affairs. I think that was why she asked for him in the first place, because they were so in tune with each other's interests.

All three of us joked and laughed as we looked at yet another terrible stain on the nursery carpet caused by William's latest Ribena attack, and Harry's latest crayon 'mural' on the day nursery wall. Diana's voice, normally flat and quite nondescript, changed as she pulled Dudley's leg about his weight. Her usual rather strangled inflection gave way to a more carefree, animated style, which only ever revealed itself with close friends.

. . .

The sound of raised voices came from the Princess's sitting room. 'You know it's the only thing I have ever wanted at Highgrove,' moaned

Diana. 'For goodness' sake, it's only a bloody tennis court.' For several months the Princess had been asking for a tennis court. And like most husbands who felt the need of a better excuse than a simple 'No', Charles had put up the excuse of expense.

'You cannot be serious,' shouted Diana, not recognising the irony of echoing John McEnroe. 'What about the thousands you pour into your precious bloody garden, and anything else which takes your fancy? I don't think you realise quite the efforts I make to go along with what you want to do all the time. What about my wants?'

This was then followed up with a warning: 'I've agreed, against my wishes, to go up to bloody Balmoral with you again, but I can still change my mind. I'm doing that for you, so why can't you do something for me for once, and not be so fucking selfish!'

I never really understood why Charles was so against his wife having her tennis court, apart from the fact that he didn't care for the game himself. Despite her complicated personality, Diana was really very simple to look after, and a gesture like that would easily have maintained some sort of status quo. A tennis court might also have encouraged her to spend more time at Highgrove, and allowed her to invite her friends over for something to do on the long-drawn-out summer days in the country.

Her warning about Balmoral was a very real threat, and in the end she refused to go on *Britannia* for the cruise of the Western Isles that always preceded the stay. She said she didn't want to go on the boat again, and as far as she was concerned her mind was made up.

It was obvious to everyone how much Diana loathed going up to Scotland anyway for the Royal Family's annual stay, and the days before any visit there were filled with tension. The place held difficult memories for her. Balmoral, and especially the Queen Mother's house, Birkhall, had been used by Charles to carry on his bachelor affairs. And although Diana's relationship with the rest of the Royal Family was still reasonably comfortable, there did seem to be an absence of real affection between her and the Queen.

Just a day before their departure in early August Diana sat in the kitchen with me, and said, 'I could really do without this holiday, Wendy. There are so many other things I should be getting on with, but I have given my word.' I told her not to worry, since no doubt she would be able to take the odd day off for a flying visit to London. The thought of that seemed to cheer her up a little, and as we drank our tea together, she quickly changed the subject to Prince William.

'Now, Wendy, you do know that you must tell him when he is being naughty,' she said, barely able to restrain her amusement at the previous day's events. William, by now quite a handful, had squirted a water pistol at a new, extremely conscientious sentry on the gate and drenched his uniform. The officer, who didn't quite know what had happened until it was too late, felt forced to remain in position for another two hours, the water running down his collar and into his shirt. William, who found the whole affair hilariously funny, continued firing until his gun was empty.

The matter had been raised unofficially by the sentry and William ticked off by his nanny. Diana, so constrained herself by the strictures of royal life, had originally laughed when told about her son's behaviour; Charles, however, had taken a very different line.

'They simply cannot do things like that,' he told his wife. 'And it makes things so much worse when they see you laughing about it.' The Prince had called William into his study for a severe dressing-down, resulting in a few moments of tears before his son was off to his next prank.

Later that afternoon the Prince asked to speak to me about a new puppy he had been promised by Lady Salisbury. 'Unfortunately I am going to be away for her first days here, Wendy,' he said. 'So Ken will bring her over tomorrow. She is a hunting terrier and I have named her Tigger. She will be Highgrove's first dog, so I hope you don't mind looking after her while I am away.' He added with a chuckle: 'No doubt the wretched thing will widdle all over the place, so if you or Paddy take her home I will naturally replace everything she ruins.'

Little Tigger, really a Jack Russell rather than the posher-sounding 'hunting terrier', was brought over by Ken Stronach the following day. And, just as Charles warned, she did 'widdle' over everything. She was very much the Prince's dog and Diana had no time for her at all. The Princess didn't seem that interested in pets unless they were for the boys, and even then her involvement was very short-lived.

Charles had arranged with Ken for large soda syphons and sheets of blotting paper to be strategically placed around the house to cope with all the mess. 'I want her to have a free run of the house so she gets used to it,' he had said. 'She will soon get house-trained if you look after her properly.'

Exactly, I thought to myself. I will be the one doing the house-training. In those first few weeks I followed her around with soda syphons clearing up puddle after puddle, and the stains on the bedroom and drawing room carpets were still there right up until I left in 1993.

. . .

I was not to see the Princess again until September, when she flew down from Scotland for poor Nesta Whiteland's funeral. I had just received notification in the morning's post that my salary was to increase from £6,070.00 to the princely sum of £6,320.00, when Joan Bodman rang to inform me of Nesta's death.

Nesta, who had stopped working at Highgrove soon after my arrival, had finally lost her long battle against cancer, and understandably Paddy was beside himself with grief. The Prince was in the middle of a trip to America and was unable to make the funeral, so Diana was flying down instead for the service at St Saviour's in Tetbury.

Colin Trimming, the Prince's detective, arrived on September 4 to check all the security arrangements. Diana arrived the next day, dressed in black and looking extremely depressed. Although she was glad to be away from Balmoral she had hoped it would be in different circumstances.

She took hold of Paddy's arm as they walked into the small country church, and for about an hour all their differences seemed to evaporate. Whatever the Princess's feeling towards her husband's long-standing supporter, Diana behaved with tremendous grace and sympathy. Her gentleness and genuine concern for Paddy were very touching, albeit surprising considering their normal relationship, which was far from comfortable.

My son James seemed concerned and apprehensive about going up to Balmoral, and I asked him what was wrong. He had been on the phone to the other travelling staff up there and had been warned that the rows between Charles and Diana had reached an all-time high. 'It's making life very difficult, apparently,' he told me quietly. 'Nobody quite knows what to do about it. The Princess has even had a psychiatrist flown up on a couple of occasions to try and work through their problems.'

Once again I realised how expertly Diana could act when carrying out her public performances, proving what a professional she was at hiding her true feelings. The fact that beneath her caring and sympathetic character at the funeral she was still going through terrible emotional problems spoke volumes about her sense of duty and keeping up appearances.

James added: 'You know, Mum, I'm not sure how much longer I want to carry on working for this family. It's all going to go very wrong sooner or later.' Neither of us realised at the time how accurate this was.

Three days later the Prince sent for Paddy. According to James, Charles took his faithful servant out every day for long fishing and walking trips. The hours spent together confirmed Paddy's role as surrogate father figure for the Prince. Paddy, an old, uncomplicated countryman, seemed to touch a chord with Charles that his own father never discovered. And on his return Paddy told me that many things had been discussed as they wandered the estate, and that the Prince had poured out his heart regarding Diana and the state of his marriage.

When Diana finally returned on September 20 I could see the pain and frustration in her eyes. The summer holidays had also involved a visit to Majorca with King Juan Carlos of Spain, but the Princess still looked drained and depressed. She showed no interest in the changes to the house and asked to have supper in her room.

Charles, uncomfortable and more difficult than ever before, had a fit when he saw the state of the cellars. 'I thought I had asked for these to be cleared of ALL the junk,' he seethed, clenching his fists tightly as he literally jumped up and down. 'Just get rid of it all. I simply cannot stand all this mess any more.' A lot of stuff was disposed of in the usual way. A few silver services and more valuable wedding presents were packed up and never seen again. It was as if they were trying to eradicate all signs of a happier past, as they came to grips with the pain and sadness of the present.

. . .

As autumn set in, and the oaks and willows around Highgrove changed from green to russet brown, the rows subsided and the Waleses settled down to a long, hard emotional winter. On the outside they both carried on with their normal duties and engagements, but at home, at Highgrove, they were locked in a bitter war of hatred.

One day I plucked up the courage to ask Diana if she was all right. I could hear her crying on the stairs by the butler's pantry, and decided that I should at least offer to comfort her. 'Thank you, Wendy,' she repeated several times. 'But I don't think you would understand. Everything is such a mess and so complicated. I just don't know what to do.'

One day as I walked through the kitchen I could hear the sound of retching in the downstairs loo. At first I thought it must have been one of the staff, so I hung around in the passageway until he or she came out to see if they wanted any help. After a couple of minutes I heard the flush go, and the turn of the key in the lock. Diana, her eyes streaming, walked out wiping her mouth with a small piece of pink tissue. She gave me a thin smile before walking slowly up to her room.

It was the first time I had seen or heard her being ill, and at the time I had no idea that the Princess was suffering from bulimia. In the past I had noticed the occasional trace of vomit when I cleaned the basin and loo in her bathroom, but had not thought any more about it. However, I talked to Ev that evening when she came down to the Lodge for a drink. 'It happens all the time,' she said darkly. 'Especially when the Princess is under a lot of pressure or particularly upset.'

The next time I went to clean her bathroom I became more aware that it was happening on a regular basis. Diana was very considerate about it, and would try to clear everything up, but still I knew what had happened, since it was my job to know every inch of the rooms in that house.

I looked at her contraceptive pills in the mug by the side of the sink, and wondered if perhaps she was pregnant, and this was merely the first sign of morning sickness. But no, the pills appeared to have been taken daily according to the instructions on the packet. I grew more alarmed when I realised this. Certainly any pills she was taking would be rendered totally useless if she was bringing everything up once a day.

Diana's vomiting began to take on a regular pattern. Every day after lunch she would go up to her room, she said to brush her teeth, but often to be sick. It wasn't as if she was eating a lot at mealtimes – her appetite was small, and she fluctuated between eating something light and sometimes barely anything at all. She would often just move the food around on her plate rather than eat it, which meant it was simply thrown out after the meal.

In early October the Prince returned to Scotland again to stay with friends at the Queen Mother's house, Birkhall. Diana, who had been slightly brighter for a few days, was once again plunged into the blackest of moods, and began to set about her dresser Evelyn in the most brutal way. She found fault with absolutely everything Ev did. The trouble was that Ev did all her work extremely well, so she knew the onslaughts were just an excuse for attacking her personally. She would often appear downstairs close to tears after having been called up to see Diana, who could be heard shouting and cursing her.

Evelyn was one of the most loyal and discreet servants Diana or any other royal could have hoped for. She had been with the Princess right from the early days and had travelled the world with her. Her work was, if anything, too immaculate. And she would never have said a word against 'the boss'.

One evening Diana rang through to the pantry and demanded that Ev went up to her room immediately. I could clearly hear Diana screaming: 'Look at this fucking shirt, Evelyn. Look at it, you idiot. It's rubbish. Rubbish, rubbish, rubbish,' she repeated over and over again. 'What is it, Evelyn? Rubbish.'

Evelyn, in her Midlands accent, would never have dared answer back. All she could say was, 'Sorry, Mam, I really am so sorry,' before Diana imperiously repeated, 'Rubbish' and shouted, 'Get out of my sight.' I walked along the corridor to Ev's room, where I found her crying on her bed. 'It's not the work I do, it can't be. It must be me, for some reason,' she sobbed.

In the end Diana's outbursts were so frequent that someone, I'm still not sure who, mentioned something to Colonel Creasy. He brought the subject up the next time I saw him.

'You know, Wendy,' he said quietly, 'as Comptroller of the Household I do know what is going on and how people are being treated. In fact I have talked to the Princess about the way she is treating Evelyn, as I'm sure you, like many others, have been very concerned about it. Evelyn is a very loyal and good dresser, and the Princess must appreciate that she is very lucky to have someone like her to work for the Household. I really will not tolerate these outbursts. The Princess cannot treat people like this and get away with it.'

Colonel Creasy was to retire several months later. I was shocked and surprised to hear him talk so candidly, and thought that perhaps the matter had been raised at the highest level for him to mention it. I decided not to say anything further, but thought secretly how cruel and vindictive Diana was being to her personal staff. I knew she had a difficult, high-profile job, and was caught in an unhappy marriage. I also accepted that, as a daughter of an Earl, she was a Lady in her own right, and entitled to certain airs and graces. What I could not accept, however, was her venom and spite when it came to humiliating defenceless people around her.

The fact that Diana, so sweet and caring on the outside and to the general public at large, was also capable of wounding sarcasm and spitefulness, not only annoyed but infuriated me. It was as if she was starting to turn into some sort of media monster, who cared only about how she came across to the public, without giving a thought to those who had to live with and work for her.

I never had a serious run-in with the Princess – I have a feeling she would never have dared. The job was not so important to me that I was prepared to take the abuse that Evelyn received. I think Diana realised that, and as a result steered clear of any confrontation as far as I was concerned.

. . .

Prince Charles seemed more able to accept the silent tension than the occasions when Diana was reduced to floods of tears. When that happened Charles was completely unable to cope. He would wring his hands in frustration and say, 'What is it now, Diana? What have I said now to make you cry?' In the end I believe he felt there was nothing that he could do or say to change things, and he would therefore ignore the outbursts.

There were many evenings when we would hear the sitting-room door bang shut, and count the steps as Diana fled to her room. A cry of 'Hard hats' or 'Action stations' would come from one of the police in the room at the time, while Ev would shake her head sadly.

As the year ran through to its bitter end, the only brief moment of happiness seemed to be a visit by Diana's sister Jane with her husband Sir Robert Fellowes and their family. Charles was away again, and with her sister Diana seemed able to relax for the first time in months. They spent hours talking together and playing with the children, organising games in the garden and taking film after film of snapshots.

Diana seemed at her happiest with the young children, and especially Jane's daughters Eleanor and Laura. I often thought she would have liked a daughter of her own. Had Charles been prepared to have another child, it might have saved the marriage as far as Diana was concerned. Another baby, especially a daughter, might have lifted her out of the despair and depression that so often engulfed her.

The Prince was growing increasingly hermetic, and reluctant to rejoin his wife in London at Kensington Palace. Gradually he tried to arrange for more of his meetings to be held at Highgrove, and to plan travel to engagements from the house.

The acting continued in public, and that year's Christmas party at the Carlton Tower Hotel in London was a marital *tour de force*. There were smiles and jokes from both of them as they circulated around the various tables. Diana began to pop balloons during Charles's speech, which raised a cheer.

'Is it time for me to stop?' said Charles as the laughter died down. 'But before I do I want you all to know how important you are to Diana and me. Isn't that right, darling?' he added as he turned towards her.

For Evelyn and those of us who were living through their problems, the words were beginning to sound a little hollow.

1987

CHAPTER SIX

Camilla

Prince Charles was taking an early evening bath. It was eight o'clock on a Sunday and I could hear the sound of the hot water pipes rumbling and shaking as he added yet more water to the bath. Diana and the nursery had returned to London straight after lunch, leaving the Prince alone, save for his detective, chef and valet, at Highgrove.

His personal detective Andy Crichton was in the staff dining room, hurriedly finishing an apple crumble Mervyn had prepared for supper. 'I'm off with the Prince again tonight,' he explained to someone who mentioned how smart he looked. 'Another private dinner engagement.' The rest of the room went quiet.

Shortly before 8.30pm Charles appeared in the hall. He looked very dapper in his jacket, open-necked shirt and cravat, and had obviously washed his hair, since he smelt strongly of soap and spicy shampoo.

'Ready then, Andrew?' he asked impatiently as Andy waited for him by the door, the car, its engine running, outside. Quietly the four-wheel drive Ford pulled away. 'Now I wonder where he is off to?' said one of the girls who had come in to wash up. 'It can't be for dinner, because he has already eaten.' Nobody answered. Because everyone knew.

Camilla Parker Bowles had been a girlfriend of Prince Charles many years before he even considered Diana as a potential bride. Though married to the Prince's friend Brigadier Andrew Parker Bowles, and the mother of his two children, Camilla tended to spend most of the week at their mansion, Middlewick House, her husband passing the week in the barracks or at their London house. Middlewick House was a twenty-minute drive from Highgrove.

At first only the detectives knew of Charles's nocturnal visits, and, as loyal servants, would never have betrayed the trust placed in them by the heir to the throne. Charles would kiss Diana and the children good-bye on Sunday afternoons, and then fix up his evening ahead. The arrangement was long-standing, and eventually word was to leak out about the 'special' friendship that still existed between the former girlfriend and the Prince.

Faithful Paddy was frequently called on to deliver notes and packages to her as she waited alone in her house. These would often be accompanied by flowers, picked by the Prince from the gardens or greenhouses, or chocolates procured by his valet. I don't think it ever occurred to Charles that he was compromising others; his position and upbringing meant that everyone obeyed his command, and his demands were always met.

Charles's secret visits were let further out of the bag by Camilla's housekeeper, a personal friend of the Highgrove groom Marion Cox, who excitedly kept a note of the number of visits made by the Prince to her employer.

'Do you know he was there by himself with Camilla for over five hours yesterday,' Marion relayed to us one weekday afternoon. 'My friend was told she could have an early day, but stayed behind anyway as they went off together. It really is a bit strange, don't you think?'

The secret trysts continued, and in the early days were usually away from Highgrove, either at Camilla's house or at the homes of mutual friends. Apart from the obvious deceit to his wife, which was a problem for those staff who understood what was going on, the visits, occasionally made at the last minute after a quick telephone call, also played havoc with the day-to-day running of the house. Because of the ridiculously strict rules for the household when the Prince was in residence, the trips would keep me awake at night, since my Lodge looked directly over the main gates.

Despite the fact that most of us knew where he was going, Diana still seemed blissfully ignorant of her husband's movements. But she was beginning to have her suspicions. One Sunday evening she rang through to the pantry from London and asked to speak to Charles. Thinking on my feet, I told her that the Prince had just popped out for a while, but would no doubt be back later on.

'Which car is he in, Wendy?' she snapped slightly hysterically. I told her the Ford. The phone went dead. Later on, I heard she had rung Charles on the car's mobile phone immediately after speaking to me, and that she and the conversation had been heated.

The first major change to affect Highgrove in 1987 was the parting of the ways for Barbara Barnes as William and Harry's nanny. The tension and animosity between the Princess and Barbara had risen noticeably over the Christmas period, and it came as no surprise when on Thursday January 15, 1987, we were told in a phone call from Kensington Palace that Barbara was leaving.

I was never to see her again, although Olga Powell, her deputy, who came with Diana and the nursery the day after the announcement, explained she had been reluctant to leave. 'It was obvious it was all going to end in tears right from the early days,' she said with a faint smile. 'As you know, Wendy, I like Barbara enormously, but her style of nannying was never going to fit in with the way the Princess wanted.'

Olga explained that Diana was a very jealous mother who, as soon as she felt she was losing control of her children, would step in to re-assert her authority. 'Barbara wanted to run everything in the nursery, and when the Prince and Princess were away she could,' she added. 'It almost got to the stage where Diana felt she had to make an appointment to see her sons, and she wasn't having any of that.'

I smiled as I remembered Barbara, head held high and dressed in a smart skirt and blouse covered by a waxed Barbour jacket, demanding to use the front door at Highgrove. 'I am entitled to use this door because I am the royal nanny,' she explained with a grin, and always did, even though Diana and the boys always made do with the back entrance. In fact, the only other people to use the front door, apart from official guests, were the Prince and Camilla.

Only a few months earlier Barbara had told me that she loved her job, but was unhappy about how difficult the Princess could be. Diana's habit of being friendly, chatty and open one day, only to cut you dead the following, did not go down well with Barbara, who called the Princess's behaviour 'downright rude'. And she also seemed concerned about the Queen's remark one Easter that William was getting a little out of control. 'His behaviour was only natural for a boy in front of his grandmother,' explained Barbara. 'What was she expecting for God's sake, a mini Prince Charles!'

However, I knew that as far as Diana was concerned, Barbara's departure was certainly for the best. After all, anything that made the Princess happier should, in the long run, I reasoned, make her easier to work for.

Olga, who had gladly worked as Barbara's deputy because she was not prepared to take on the job full-time, explained that the announcement was timed to coincide with Prince William's first day at Wetherby School in Notting Hill Gate. But she added that, when told Barbara was leaving, William seemed extremely upset.

'He wasn't the only one,' she said. 'You know what Barbara felt about William. She would have done anything for that child. The trouble is that Diana obviously feels the same way, and felt her mother's prerogative was being threatened.'

Olga dismissed as complete fabrication press reports that Diana had been angry about Barbara's trip to Mustique with her former employer Lord Glenconner, Princess Margaret, Roddy Llewellyn, Raquel Welch and Jerry Hall. 'Barbara asked the Princess months in advance if she could go on that,' said Olga, 'and was told it was absolutely fine.'

For several weeks after Barbara left, Diana decided to look after the boys herself at weekends. Perhaps as a way of re-establishing her importance in the day-to-day running of their lives, she took great delight in bathing and dressing them, something she felt to be important both to herself and to them. Fortunately, William appeared to be loving school, and was as playful and noisy as ever. Harry, who was becoming more independent by the day, still looked up to his older brother to take the initiative in their games, but was already beginning to prove himself the superior horseman when it came to putting Smokey through his paces.

.   .   .

The sound of breaking china carried through the downstairs passageway and into the kitchen, followed by muffled shouting. 'Don't read the bloody things if you don't like what they say,' shouted Charles as Diana tried to pick up the broken pieces of a cup and saucer from the floor. 'It's all rubbish anyway. You only make things ten times worse by playing into their hands.'

Diana, her eyes filling with tears, snapped back: 'What do you mean, play into their hands? I do what I do as much for you and your bloody family as for myself. It's me they want to see anyway, and you know that as well as I do.'

Charles gave a dismissive chuckle as he turned the pages of his *Sunday Times*. 'Oh really? Do you honestly think that?' Turning to one of the tabloid papers that had sparked Diana's outburst, he read: 'Difficult Di causes malice at the Palace', then added, 'Sounds about right to me.'

The Princess let out a scream, pushed her chair back and ran out of the room straight into Prince William, who had wandered down to the dining room after hearing all the noise. 'What's the matter, Mummy?' he asked as Diana scooped him up in her arms and carried him off to her bedroom. 'Why are you crying?'

Diana's fascination with her publicity was a double-edged sword. When something flattering was written about her, or a particularly good set of pictures taken, she would be on cloud nine for hours. But when a critical piece appeared she would often fly into an hysterical rage. The fire-grates were often filled with the remnants of unflattering articles about her.

Charles took the opposite line, believing that if you didn't read the criticism it would not affect you. There were times, however, when articles were faxed over to him from his office, if something particularly bad or shocking had been written. These were then read and tossed angrily on to the fire. 'Bloody gutter press,' he would grumble. 'Why can't they just leave us alone?'

Ever the countryman, Prince Charles was trying to make the best use of the local hunts around Highgrove. He loved the thrill of the sport, and the friends he made out on the field. Paddy would often ring around to fix up the horses, and travel with the Prince to whichever hunt he was joining that day.

Charles's hunting days followed a set pattern that rarely altered. Very much a slave to routine, he would get up at the usual time and come down for breakfast in his breeches, shirt and waistcoat, and thick socks. But as well as his usual frugal meal of herb bread and tea with honey he would also ask for a special salad roll, which he would usually take with him in his lunchbox and eat during the day until hunting tea at about 5pm.

When he had to travel by car to the hunts in Derbyshire, Charles would usually take a packed lunchbox filled with a roll, fruit and maybe some oatmeal biscuits. It also contained a bottle of his favourite lemon refresher, made by the chef every day, and some individual cartons of apple juice. It always amused me to think of the Prince driving along the motorway, eating his sandwiches and drinking apple juice through a straw like any other ordinary man in the street.

After the day's hunting, Charles would usually be invited back to a fellow huntsman's home for tea. Occasionally, however, he invited people he met out on the field back to Highgrove for boiled eggs and whisky. When this happened, his detective would ring ahead on the mobile phone to give us advance warning of the numbers expected. I knew that Charles wanted his eggs cooked for three minutes exactly, and that Mervyn usually had several lots on the go to ensure that at least one batch was perfect. The others were simply thrown away.

On this particular day, when the chefs were off duty, the Prince returned home at a quarter past five, his distinctive navy-blue riding coat with special Prince of Wales buttons, nicknamed the 'conductor's coat' because it made him look like a bus conductor, spattered in mud. He had invited two guests.

Expecting the others to arrive any minute, I waited a little and then put six eggs into the pan of boiling water. Three minutes passed and still no guests had arrived. Charles paced up and down the hall, muttering.

I looked at my first batch of eggs, took them out of the water and threw them away, before putting another lot on. Fifteen minutes and three more sets of eggs later the other huntsmen finally arrived. Charles, polite as ever, did not even mention their delay but invited them straight through to the dining room. There, to my great relief, they sat down and asked for boiled eggs.

Seconds later, to their great surprise, the last six remaining eggs in the kitchen – cooked to perfection for three minutes each – were immediately rushed through and deposited on the table. Now that's royal service for you, I thought.

. . .

With the Prince and Princess constantly travelling, the valets and dressers needed to lug vast quantities of clothes around to cover any eventuality. They were away in Portugal from February 11 to 14, and skiing with Andrew and Sarah in Switzerland the following Monday. I had never seen their travelling staff so rushed off their feet.

In advance of the trips all the clothes were laid out on the beds in the Blue and Green rooms for the Prince and Princess to inspect before each garment was carefully wrapped in tissue paper and packed in large trunks. The respective valet and dresser would also be responsible for hand-washing the royal boxer shorts and panties, and theoretically nobody else was allowed to touch them. Nevertheless, it would be left to me sometimes to unload from the Highgrove washing machine Charles's plain white boxer shorts, and Diana's Sea Island white cotton bras and panties. Both Diana and the Prince were fastidious about the state of their underwear, and as soon as anything looked grey or too worn, it was replaced.

Both of them went meticulously through their changes of clothing for the trips and Diana demanded a new set of ski wear, commenting, 'I can't wear the same things every day, can I?' to Evelyn as she looked at the vast selection of clothes on the bed.

As the royal couple frolicked around on the ski-slopes of Klosters, and went their separate ways in the evenings – Diana choosing to taste the resort's night life, Charles to read – Highgrove carried on as weekend home for the boys. Olga and the nursery arrived with the boys' detective Ken Wharfe.

It was the first time that I had met Ken, who was later to be taken on as Diana's personal protection officer, and I was completely charmed by his wonderful sense of fun. He was a great opera fan, and spent the weekend prancing around the kitchen bellowing out arias in his light baritone, as we prepared the meals for the boys and the staff. William and Harry loved him. His sense of humour was terrific and he always had them in fits of laughter as he tried to teach them to tap-dance on the hall floor. Apparently his aunt had taught him as a young teenager, and Ken said it stood him in good stead for life as a royal detective.

That Friday evening Diana and Charles rang from Switzerland to say goodnight to the boys, who by now were so exhausted that they could barely keep their eyes open. Olga had everything completely under control. When William shouted that he didn't want to do something she would rebuke him sternly, then cut in just before the tears started with, 'It's only because I love you, William, that I am being so strict.' This, followed by a kiss, usually got her what she wanted with the minimum of fuss.

There was a hard and fast rule that no nanny was allowed to slap the children unless they had been exceptionally rude. Poking a tongue out didn't always count, but deliberate spitting and disobeying rules did. It rarely happened at Highgrove, where the boys were not on show. It was only outside that William in particular felt the need to test the water to see how far his bad behaviour could go.

Olga was proud of her position as deputy nanny to the princes. But she worried about how their lives would develop surrounded by such tremendous publicity wherever they went. 'It can't be good for them, being followed around by photographers wherever they go for the rest of their lives,' she would complain every time their pictures appeared in the papers. 'Look how it affects their mother.'

That afternoon another royal car arrived at the back door. Princess Anne's daughter Zara Phillips jumped out and ran in, shouting 'hello' as she entered. Zara, a toothy youngster, had come for tea with William and Harry, and all the children raced up to the nursery with Olga. Like both princes, Zara had an impish sense of fun and there were soon shrieks of laughter coming from the nursery. William was making gargling noises with his jelly, and letting it dribble down his chin, despite Olga's best endeavours. Zara joined in, as did Harry, and soon there was pandemonium upstairs. I went to help Olga clear up after they had all quietened down in front of the video. When all else failed a video was usually the only way of restoring peace.

Zara left with her detective soon after tea. Like all royal children, she had exquisite manners. As she walked down the stairs she came up to me and said, 'Thank you very much for having me, Wendy,' before stepping into the car that was taking her back to Gatcombe Park.

Like any young boys, William and Harry needed constant attention and an action-packed schedule to stop them getting bored. With this in mind, Diana had arranged for them to go for lunch with Lord and Lady Vestey's children the following day, to fill the last few hours before their parents returned. They were already back when the boys, with Ken and Olga, came up the drive. Ken let William toot the horn at Diana as she stood by the front door waiting to greet them. She looked absolutely radiant, her skin lightly tanned and her eyes sparkling with excitement as her two children jumped out of the car and into her arms.

That evening the family had a special tea of crumpets and cakes together in front of a roaring fire in the sitting room, the boys fascinated by a toy railway set delivered by London Underground earlier that day. Charles and Diana seemed more relaxed together than I had seen them for ages. I was beginning to think that, with a bit of hard work, everything might be all right after all.

CHAPTER SEVEN

The Art of Scoring Points

The Princess rang through to the pantry from her sitting room. 'Do you know what time the Prince is coming back?' she asked somewhat tetchily. 'I thought we were meant to be having supper together this evening.'

Charles had left early that morning to hunt with a pack of hounds several hours' drive away from Highgrove. Paddy had gone with him, and as it was now 7.45pm we were all wondering what had happened to them. I told her we would have heard if there had been a puncture or accident, and that unfortunately the PPO's mobile phone was still out of range, either because they were in hilly countryside, or because it had accidentally been switched off.

'So inconsiderate,' muttered Diana before hanging up. I could feel the storm clouds gathering, and gave a secret prayer that Charles would return soon. Mervyn did not seem too bothered, however. The food for their supper was all prepared and just waiting to go into the microwave.

Shortly before 9pm Paddy, Charles and his detective arrived, the Prince appearing at the main door with a slightly pained expression due to a minor fall that afternoon. He went straight through to his study and rang for some tea and whisky. Seconds later I heard the door of the Princess's sitting room slam shut and Diana run down the stairs. She barged past James, who was in the passageway with the Prince's tea things, and dashed straight into the room where Charles was sitting in an armchair. 'Where the hell have you been?' she asked. 'I was worried sick something had happened to you.'

Charles, who appeared slightly bemused by her appearance, replied with a non-committal, 'If anything serious had happened you would have heard, darling. We just got a bit held up.'

'What about the supper we were meant to be having together?' she retorted. 'I don't suppose you remember that, do you? I'm not important enough for you to remember arrangements like that.' As James left the room, Charles was trying to explain that he had asked some friends over for a drink that evening. 'They are charming people,' he continued. 'I am sure you will love them.'

'Stuff your friends,' shouted Diana. 'If you can't make time for your wife, I am certainly not making time for your cronies.' With that, she walked out and stomped off to her room.

Both obviously raced for the phones at the same time, one call from the Prince asking James to prepare a drinks tray for two guests, the other from the Princess asking for a supper tray.

When the Prince's friends eventually arrived, they were ushered into the pale yellow sitting room. 'I'm afraid my wife has a headache and has had an early night,' said Charles, his face betraying not a hint of the previous argument, as his guests plumped down in the white, yellow and violet chintz chairs. 'She sends her apologies and hopes she can meet you another time.'

It was the first of many occasions when Diana refused to come down and meet her husband's friends for a drink or a meal. It soon became obvious to them what was going on, but it never ceased to amaze me how the Prince could switch so effortlessly from an angry domestic tiff to a calm social situation in a matter of seconds. It must have come from years of training!

The fact that he had either forgotten or simply didn't care about being late for dinner with his wife was typical of the Prince's occasional off-hand manner with Diana. Though scrupulously polite with her, and with most people, he still possessed a core of selfishness undoubtedly born of his privileged lifestyle. If he was enjoying himself on the hunting field or polo ground, and was not obliged to go on to an official engagement, he was quite prepared to jettison previous arrangements to pursue the fun of the present. Such an attitude drove Diana to despair, and led to the most fearful rows and black depressions.

Paul Burrell, formerly one of the Queen's footmen at Buckingham Palace, had recently joined us as butler at Highgrove. Although he had seen the Prince and Princess at first hand before, he was nevertheless surprised by the chaotic state of their marriage. 'I suppose I just carry on, even if they are in mid-fight,' he joked one evening after a series of spectacularly loud slamming doors. 'I am sure that is what the Queen would expect.'

Paul, a chubby and friendly character, was to become one of the Princess's closest allies over the years ahead. The Queen, who unlike some other members of the Royal Family was immensely respected by all the staff, had been reluctant to let him go, but was happy that Paul and his wife Maria, who had worked as Prince Philip's maid, could rear a family in the country. 'The Queen was and is the most gracious of the whole lot of them,' my son James told me. 'She doesn't really have a different private side from her public persona. She was always scrupulously polite and charming, and would pause if she had time to have a quiet word as she passed you. It never amounted to more than "How are you, James?" and would never be uttered if she was with guests, but it was still more than Prince Philip would do, or others like Prince Andrew and later Fergie, who would often walk around as if nobody else was there.'

James also remembered the Queen's kindness and loyalty to old retainers in other royal residences, some of whom were over-fond of the bottle. 'One of the royal yeomen had been celebrating a bit too liberally one evening and decided to take a little snooze on the back stairs. Normally this would not have mattered too much, since the royals do not use these stairs. For some reason, that evening the Queen decided to walk that way – looking for a bowl for one of the corgis, I think – and came across the crumpled heap emitting highly alcoholic vapours and loud snores. The Queen had to step over him and came into one of the back rooms to speak quietly to the Serjeant. "I think Mr So-and-So might need a hand," she whispered. Nothing else was ever said about the incident – there were no reprimands and certainly no threats or cautions. This incident essentially showed the Queen for what she is – fair and prepared to give people a chance.'

· · ·

Paul's arrival coincided with the appointment of a new nanny for William and Harry. Formerly a Great Ormond Street nurse, Ruth Wallace arrived with the boys at Highgrove on Friday March 13, 1987. Extrovert, witty and great fun, Ruth was clearly going to be a great hit with the staff as well as the boys. Unlike Olga, who always ate with the boys in the nursery, Ruth made it clear she was going to have her meals with the rest of the staff, and join in with the pre- and post-dinner drinks.

It was obvious from the start that Ruth, an attractive, vivacious girl, had an eye for the men. A born storyteller, she appealed to the detectives' sense of fun, and spent many a convivial evening with them.

'I can see we're going to have some fun and games with that one,' observed Paddy that first weekend. 'But she looks as if she can take good care of herself. Let's see how long she can cope with the Princess.'

Diana came through to the dining room where I was looking at the state of the covers on the chairs. Over the last few months they had become worn and tatty, having been used by William and Harry, now better behaved, for the occasional breakfast and lunch with their parents.

The Princess, dressed in a long heavy skirt and flat shoes, had no make-up on but still looked fantastic, her slightly damp hair pulled tightly back. She thanked me for getting her showerhead fixed the previous week.

It was this inconsistency in Diana that made her so infuriatingly difficult to work for. One day she would make a point of coming to thank you for a minor chore like repairing a shower, the next, after you had really gone out of your way to do something for her, she would cut you, a million miles away in her thoughts. I, like most staff, did not expect continuous thanks, but whereas Charles was consistently polite and considerate to everyone, Diana was not.

. . .

As a general rule Charles and Diana tried to make Highgrove their weekend base, turning down invitations to other friends' houses and inviting them instead to Gloucestershire. In the first few months of 1987 there were overnight stays by Sarah Keswick, daughter of the Earl of Dalhousie and wife of millionaire banker Chippendale 'Chips' Keswick, the Fellowes family, and Sarah Ferguson, by now the Duchess of York.

The Prince was not always present at these weekends, since, unlike Diana, he would often go abroad for three or four days at a time on private visits. His fascination with Europe, and Italy in particular, made Charles read everything he possibly could about the country. One of his favourite after-dinner conversations was about the civilising aspects of the Italian people.

He once asked me if I knew anything about Leonardo da Vinci. I replied that I had studied him briefly at A level. He stopped, did a double-take, and then said, 'A levels, did you say, Wendy?' When I told him that I had a degree, he coughed and, looking me straight in the eye, added conspiratorially: 'If you are so well qualified then why on earth are you here? Why are you working as a housekeeper?'

I didn't think the Prince had even considered that his staff were of a higher form of academic life than the brain-dead. He laughed when I told him that several of us had quite good qualifications. 'Good grief,' he replied. 'I didn't know everyone was so brainy around here.'

. . .

By all accounts the Prince and Princess's stay at Windsor that Easter was a disaster. Gossip on the Royal Household grapevine went into overdrive as stories about the couple's indifference to each other reached even the lowliest housemaid and stable-hand. The telephone in the pantry kept on ringing after they had left Windsor, with anxious staff asking if their behaviour was as bad at Highgrove. One caller, a footman at Windsor for the Easter break, asked if Charles was seeing anyone else. 'It's as if Diana is deliberately setting out to punish him for something,' he added. 'God help us if Charles is being a naughty boy and going on a trip down memory lane with his old flames. The way the Princess is behaving at the moment, I wouldn't put anything past her.'

That May the couple were reunited at Highgrove. Diana, fed up by the lack of time and attention given to her by Charles, was at her worst. Her early morning swims were followed by hours alone with the children in the gardens or watching videos in her sitting room. At other times she would take off by herself and not tell anyone where she was going. 'It's going to have to stop,' said one of the policemen over supper that night. 'She can't just drive away into the outside world without explaining where she is going. She should know that by now.'

Charles, however, did not seem to care, leaving it to the police or personal staff to try to prevent these solitary excursions. He was too wrapped up in his polo and garden to notice the upheaval, often spending hours away from the house and his unhappy marriage.

With the tension rising, staff felt under increasing stress. My son James, fed up with the atmosphere and stifling selfishness of both the Prince and Princess, decided he could take no more, and handed in his resignation on May 20. We had a long discussion the evening before about what he was going to do.

'It's been fun for a while, Mum, although I did rather resent having to jump to it for the equerries and private secretaries. I thought royal service was going to mean just that,' he said rather incredulously. 'But the court and hangers-on took up more of our time than the family itself.' The courtiers, usually chinless wonders with a family connection somewhere, were treated to a lifestyle that went out with the Raj. At Buckingham Palace there was a hotline straight to the footmen's room and butlers' pantry – they had to be addressed as Sir and Madam because of their position, and the staff were often admonished if they were as much as two minutes late. People like Mr Fellowes were typical of the lot of them – polite but ever so unctuous. In the order of things he was up there close to Royalty – so he made sure he got every privilege he could. The below-stairs staff were invisible unless their white gloves happened to be grubby – THEN they heard all about it.

James added, 'You know, I've got to the stage where I just cannot respect the Prince and Princess any more. Their unhappy lives are destroying my own, and I don't want to be caught in the crossfire.'

The crossfire James talked about was even more evident the second week in June, when the Prince and Princess arrived at Highgrove for a week's stay. Neither appeared able to do anything without annoying the other, and the tetchiness and resentment they felt seemed to infect the whole house.

Both took long phone calls from friends around the country: Charles from his old friend Lady Tryon, whom he called Kanga, and Camilla Parker Bowles; Diana from girl and bachelor friends from her single days, including Major David Waterhouse and a banker friend, Philip Dunne. We were told not to pick up the phone whenever it went on her personal line, but to notify her immediately, wherever she was. Occasionally this meant rushing into the garden to let her know, the phone loudly ringing out in her room all the while. We also had a large brass bell by the pantry door that we could ring to let them know that a phone call was waiting. Diana would drop whatever she was doing and dart back inside the house to take the call, sometimes appearing as much as an hour later, her face wreathed in smiles.

On polo days Charles would appear at breakfast in his dazzling white polo breeches and shirts. Sometimes his polo manager, Major Ronald Ferguson, drove over to discuss tactics before the match; at other times the Prince would drive over to the ground with his detective in his green Aston Martin and have his pep talk with him there. Ferguson was usually on the phone every day during the polo season.

William and Harry used to get terribly excited when they saw Charles dressed for polo and plead to be allowed to accompany him. The Prince was visibly delighted when this happened, saying he would love them to attend the match, as long as they kept away from the ponies. However, the boys' wishes were not always fulfilled. It depended very much on Diana's mood at the time. Some days she acquiesced – even though she detested polo and the accompanying social spectacle – but at other times she explained that alternative arrangements had been made.

Paul and I were beginning to notice the start of a power play over the boys between the Prince and Princess. While undoubtedly arrangements had been made on certain days, it was nevertheless patently obvious on other occasions that Diana was putting up excuses and pretexts. 'Oh, I'm sorry, darlings,' she would say to the boys. 'But I did promise Maria that I would take you over to visit this afternoon. You can go to polo another time.'

When no other excuse was available, Diana might reluctantly agree to take the boys to one of their father's matches. Yet even there the power battle was evident, intensely annoying Charles in the process. One morning, after a particularly strenuous game the previous day, which had been attended by most of the world's press, Charles was infuriated to see the papers full of pictures of Diana stretched out in the grass, with young Prince Harry playing quietly beside her. There were no pictures of Charles at all, despite the fact that he had scored several goals.

Diana smiled smugly as she looked through the papers, saying to her husband: 'Look, darling, at these pictures of me and your son. Aren't they good?' Charles, in shirtsleeves and old cotton trousers, cast a quick glimpse at the photos. 'Quite the little glamour model, aren't you,' he muttered before leaving the table and walking into the garden.

. . .

The gardens were still the Prince's pride and joy, and most visits included a tour of the estate – either long or short, depending on the interest shown. Fergie, more light-hearted with Charles than ever, would pull his leg gently as he offered to show his friends around the flowerbeds. 'You mean you haven't seen the roses?' she would say in mock horror when a guest politely expressed an interest. 'You mean Charles has never shown you them before?' Diana and Sarah would then collapse into fits of laughter as the guest felt obliged to walk around the garden with the Prince.

Charles's other pride and joy was the vegetable garden, his asparagus and rhubarb plots sending him into seventh heaven. Often he would pick a handful of asparagus stems on his way around and bring them into the kitchen, saying to Mervyn with a mixture of pride and humility: 'Have you seen how wonderful this asparagus is? Would you mind possibly steaming it for dinner this evening? I have a feeling it is going to be delicious.' After he had left the room, Mervyn would look at the sad little handful of vegetables and smile. 'Not a particularly healthy bunch, are you?' he would address them. 'But picked by the Prince's fair hand, so you'll do.'

Diana found her husband's eccentric love of gardening amusing at first, then intensely irritating. 'If only I were as important as his bloody garden,' she once moaned to Paul, as Charles toiled late into the warm summer evening with the gardeners.

. . .

The Prince's polo had taken a toll on his back. One morning he came down to breakfast almost bent double, his face twisted in pain. 'Oh Wendy,' he moaned, 'I can hardly move.'

The Prince's single bed had been changed earlier that year for a specially designed hand-built one with an attached valance. He had specifically asked for certain features, wanting firmer support, but was complaining that morning he needed something harder still. 'I really am going to have to get something done,' he said to Diana as she toyed with her live yoghurt over breakfast.

'Why don't you just give up polo?' she replied.

The weekend before William's fifth birthday in June, Charles and Diana attended the wedding of their mutual friend Lord Worcester to the actress Tracy Ward. Both drove in separate cars to the service and on to the reception at Cornwell Manor. As they left that morning, I could detect a strange excitement in the Princess, as if it was the first time she had come alive for months.

Although the Prince returned soon after 2am, Diana was not to return until dawn. The following morning Charles appeared at breakfast at the normal time. He looked preoccupied and fiddled nervously with a piece of toast as he waited impatiently for his tea. Diana did not surface until much later, and then spent the day alone by the pool. Not a word passed between them throughout the entire day.

'Sounds as if there was a bit of a jealous tiff last night,' laughed Ev over lunch. 'It seems that Diana was doing a bit of point-scoring at the wedding.'

The papers were full of stories about the Worcester wedding, revealing details of Diana dancing closely with her tall, handsome friend Philip Dunne, while Charles chatted conspiratorially to his old flame Anna Wallace. Apparently Charles had approached Diana halfway through a dance with Dunne, and asked her to come home with him. Diana, it was said, had laughed in his face and carried on dancing. The Prince then left 'in a huff', according to most reports.

'Sounds like a bit of one-upmanship going on there,' added one of the policemen who had come into the kitchen for a cup of coffee. 'The Prince didn't seem too happy at all.'

. . .

Prince William, by now largely over his jelly-gargling days, had handed over the mantle of royal rascal to his younger brother Harry. Aged five on June 21, William was treated to a party thrown by his mother while Charles thrashed away on the polo field.

That evening Princess Anne's Scimitar car pulled up in the back courtyard with Anne at the wheel, and a detective beside her. Dressed informally in jeans and a cotton shirt and with her hair tied back in a loose ponytail, the Princess looked marvellous. I had not realised how slim and attractive she was when away from her official public duties. She looked in on me in the kitchen as she walked through to the hall.

'Hello, it's Wendy, isn't it?' she said as she passed. 'Zara did so enjoy her day here recently. Is my brother back yet?'

Charles, in shorts and bare-chested, was sitting on a comfortable chair in the sunshine. He got up to kiss her. 'How nice of you to call by,' he said, before ordering some Pimms for them both. Both ate an early evening dinner outside on the terrace.

Despite Diana's public statements to the contrary, she never enjoyed an easy relationship with Charles's sister. Though informal greetings came naturally, there was no real warmth between them, undoubtedly because they had nothing in common. Anne, like Charles, was a country person and shared with him an interest in horses. Diana was a city girl at heart, who could think of nothing more boring than discussing a horse's form *ad nauseam*.

Diana popped her head around the door to say hello, but politely refused the offer to join them. 'I must go and see William,' she said. 'It's his birthday, you know.'

. . .

After such a gruelling few months of friction and heartache, the annual staff barbecue on July 10 was anticipated apprehensively. However, none of us had any need to worry. The whole day passed happily, with Charles and Diana mingling with the guests and laughing aloud as if they didn't have a care in the world.

Other household staff were bussed up from London for the evening, and by 11pm the event had turned into quite a party. Drink was flowing and slowly couples went off for long romantic walks around the gardens. Charles came up to me and a group of people and talked about the wonderful scents coming from the garden that evening, before complimenting the white wine we were drinking. Someone giggled as he said how nice he thought it was. It was basically plonk, and Charles, who took no interest in wine apart from his favourite sweet Muscat de Beaumes de Venise, Domaine des Bernardins, 1989, was not fooling anyone!

The Prince would often be sent crates of wine as presents, but would not really know how good it was. This led to certain members of staff who prided themselves on their good palates making off with a few 'natural breakages' of exceptionally good wine whenever they could.

The party hotted up. Diana danced and chatted with staff she had cut as recently as the day before. Later on we were all invited down to the detectives' house, Long Furlong, to continue the party. They had put lights up in the garden and arranged a small sound system to carry on with the dancing.

The Prince and Princess were invited, but Charles, fearing that his presence might make people uneasy, declined. Diana, however, readily accepted and joined the rest of us. Charles, who thought his staff should have their own privacy, and that the firm line between staff and friends should not be broken, made a comment to Diana. She replied, 'Oh don't be so silly,' and walked away.

At Long Furlong she kicked off her shoes and danced with anyone who would join in. Some slow numbers she danced alone, gyrating to the music with a surprising determination. 'Come on, Wendy,' she shouted above the din, 'dance with me to this one.' I jigged around as she stylishly threw herself into one of the chart records that year. I told her I was getting a bit old for this sort of thing. 'No, you're not,' she cried, as the music moved to a faster tempo.

The Princess seemed at her happiest when hurling herself around the dance floor with Ken, who, knowing some fancy footwork, was able to match all her steps. None of us got to bed until dawn!

. . .

My battered old Nissan car was brought to an abrupt halt at a newly erected road block along the back drive. Two menacing soldiers stood in front of it, one of them putting up his hand and insisting I stop. 'Name,' he shouted, pointing his gun at me through the driver's window.

'Wendy Berry,' I replied timidly, secretly terrified that I had done something wrong. The other soldier, dressed in full combat gear and with his face blacked out with special camouflage paint, swaggered slowly around my car.

'Could do with a new car, if you ask me, Mrs Berry,' he hissed. 'Not a very nice car at all.' As I waited in the driver's seat the two soldiers walked to the side of the drive, deciding whether to let me past.

'Regulations say you can go through if you pay a forfeit,' shouted one of them, his oversize beret slipping hilariously to one side of his head. 'But how much?' said the other. Putting his water pistol safely back in his holster, William suggested 10 pence.

'No, 20p. It's got to be 20p,' countered Harry, running at his brother by the side of the road.

I looked through my purse. The only small change I had was a 50 pence piece. 'Will this do?' I asked nervously.

'That's fine, Wendy,' replied William. 'We'll let you off the next time.' A hand darted through the open window and grabbed the coin. 'Thank you very much.' Both boys then ran off down the drive, giggling and shouting as they raced each other back to the house.

William and Harry's forfeit blockade was one of the hazards for any visitor to Highgrove. Both boys loved this particular game, and on good days could haul in quite a fortune. They adored collecting money from unsuspecting lunch guests, and, if you were unfortunate, would hit you for another 'toll' on the way out as well. I, like most of the staff, could usually see the signs of an ambush from afar, but still played along with their game to keep them amused.

It used to be quite charming to see how delighted they were on receiving the cash. It was also interesting to see how seriously Harry, in particular, took the game. Not for him the waste of an opportunity – why make 10p profit when 20p was easily attainable?

Any attempt to escape was a very grave mistake. For the boys were usually hiding in the bushes, and on seeing someone trying to clear the path would race towards them shouting 'charge!', letting off great squirts of water from their pistols. I learned from bitter experience that unless I was armed with my own water jet – a bottle usually used for watering the plants – I would not make it back to the house without getting soaked.

Both children enjoyed harmless practical jokes. Nothing serious ever happened to their victims apart from a little loss of dignity. One day when Charles was going on an official trip in the red helicopter of the Queen's Flight he was attacked from behind by Harry, dressed in army kit. Charles, in a dark formal suit, was jumped on just yards away from the helicopter. Unfortunately for him, Harry had been rolling around earlier in the paddock and was liberally covered with sheep dung. As a result, the Prince's back was now striped wih green and black stains.

Fortunately his valet was on hand to point this out, and Charles marched back indoors for a hasty wipe-down. The damp patches on his suit were then dried with a hairdryer while the helicopter was kept waiting for a full fifteen minutes. 'Look at me!' moaned Charles as he walked back into the house, half laughing, half angry. 'I'm absolutely *covered* in sheep shit.' There were no tantrums and no recriminations. I think he could see the joke as much as the rest of us, who had to rush out every few minutes to stop ourselves laughing.

The grounds of Highgrove made a perfect adventure playground for William and Harry, who were able to run around freely without being constantly shadowed by their personal protection officers. Perhaps the most enduring of their games involved the woodshed. Here was a large net filled with thousands of multi-coloured small plastic balls, which William and Harry would dive into and 'swim' through for hours on end. The balls softened any fall and were perfect for hurling naughty young boys into when a half-serious punishment was called for. There would be shrieks of laughter as I or a policeman picked them up after a drenching from their extra-powerful water pistols, and tossed them into the shed. The added bonus was that it made us feel a lot better as well!

Although both boys enjoyed riding in the early days, it was Harry who pursued the hobby. The doctor was later to ban William from riding after he was accidentally hit over the head with a golf club at Ludgrove School. The fear was that a further injury to his skull might lead to complications later, and the decision was taken to keep him away from contact sports and potentially dangerous activities like riding. I don't think it bothered him too much, since his interest was already waning.

Like most young children, William and Harry liked to keep up with all the latest TV programmes. They were fortunate in having a TV soap addict for a mother. Had it been left to Charles – very much part of the old 'too much television is bad for you' school – neither boy would have seen more than one programme a week, and that would probably have been a documentary. Diana, however, simply adored soaps such as *Casualty* and *Angels*. She had a fascination with medical and police dramas, which often led to long conversations with the staff about the plot the following morning. Maybe that's why she shows such interest in hospital work, I thought to myself.

As in any family, there were tears if William and Harry were not allowed to watch their favourite TV programme, and Olga Powell and Ruth Wallace were both stricter than their mother in rationing the amount of television. Both boys adored videos as well, and would some-times plead to go out on Saturday afternoons to choose one in Tetbury. Diana had her own television and video in her sitting room, which meant the boys could also watch with her, and a set in her bedroom, which William in particular used to watch, tucked up in bed with her.

· · · ·

While most large country houses might require a thorough spring-clean, Highgrove needed a total de-infestation throughout the entire summer. As soon as the weather turned hot the house was completely overrun with flies, moths and maggots in the cupboards. Many of the problems arose from the ancient stockpiles of supplies stashed away in the kitchen.

It was time to call in the Highgrove moth man, Mr Daly. He stared in amazement at the amount of dry foodstuffs left lying around and warned that, if much of it wasn't destroyed immediately, he might as well pack up there and then and never bother to return.

The hoarding of food on the one hand contrasted uneasily with the terrible waste in the day-to-day running of the catering. Vast amounts of food were ordered on a daily basis, but much was never used. Mervyn had a penchant for thick, heavy cream-based sauces, and would order gallons of dairy products every week. When these went off, as they frequently did, they were tipped down the sink, causing such blockages that we were all sent memos about waste disposal.

The fridge was always stocked to its limit whenever the royals were in residence – the chefs needed extra supplies to cope with any unforeseen visit by their friends or other members of the Royal Family. On the other hand, if they ordered precise amounts for the number of guests they could be caught short.

One lunchtime, when ten guests were expected, Mervyn prepared pheasant, and allowed two pieces of breast per person. One of the visitors, a retired colonel and landowner with a hearty appetite, helped himself to four pieces, which meant someone was going to have to do without.

Paul, the butler, spotting this immediately, raced into the kitchen. 'Who is going to have to stand there and take the flak when someone doesn't get their pheasant?' he shouted at everyone. 'I'll tell you who – me. I'm going to get the blame for some almighty cock-up when it's not my fault. What do you want me to do?' he bawled at Mervyn. 'Go over to Colonel So and So and take two pieces of pheasant off his plate?' The whole scene was like something out of *Fawlty Towers*.

Mervyn looked in the fridge and saw a piece of chicken that he was saving for the dog's dinner. He whipped it out, muttering 'Sorry, Tigger,' and slammed it under the grill. 'Who's the least important guest, Paul?' he asked. 'Make sure you serve this to him.' Fortunately the guests were still busy talking and drinking, and some had not yet been served when Paul dashed in five minutes later with a very rare piece of chicken.

.   .   .

By September relations between the Prince and Princess had taken yet another turn for the worse. Diana seemed to go out of her way to irritate Charles, who would take no notice of her. She would ask deliberately obvious questions about the garden in a mock-serious tone heavily laced with sarcasm. 'Who is getting the benefit of your wisdom today?' she enquired one morning as he appeared in his old gardening clothes. 'The sheep or the raspberry bushes?' The Prince ignored her.

With yet more storm clouds brewing, Diana's mother Mrs Frances Shand Kydd came down to stay on Friday September 11; pointedly, Charles was away for the weekend. It was a thrill for the boys to have their other granny staying at Highgrove, especially in such a relaxed and informal environment. The days were spent lounging around by the pool and eating together on the terrace. William and Harry, by now able to sit at table and have a proper conversation, loved the fact that they were allowed to eat with the grown-ups.

The weekend provided Diana with a much needed tonic as well. Both mother and daughter looked sad to part on the Monday morning. Many things had obviously been discussed between them, in the absence of Prince Charles.

After the initial close friendship between Fergie and Diana, it was a surprise to find the Yorks weekending with Charles alone at the end of October. Sarah had grown to rely on Prince Charles for his advice as the fickle popular press's adoration for her began to wane. She was often on the phone to him, ringing through to the main house if she could not raise him on his personal line, asking for his comments on future projects and plans. Charles seemed genuinely fond of his sister-in-law, and admired her strong, earthy nature. It made a welcome contrast to his wife's sulks and black moods.

The Prince, Andrew and Sarah sat together in the drawing room for many hours as the rain tumbled down outside, talking from early morning right through lunch and into the late afternoon. The mood was relaxed and informal, and there seemed to be a strong common bond between them, which was not always apparent when Diana was present.

The following day Charles was off to Germany with Diana for an official tour. And judging by the initial press reports it appeared that his talks with his brother and sister-in-law had done him some good. Both the Prince and Princess seemed to be putting a brave face on things, and trying to work through their differences.

Charles seemed to be finding solace in his family, inviting Prince Edward and his girlfriend at the time, Georgie May, to Highgrove for his thirty-ninth birthday on November 14. There was a special dinner for the four of them that evening, when Charles opened cards and small gifts from his family and staff.

'Not much of a birthday party,' murmured the girl washing up in the kitchen. 'There don't seem to be that many laughs, at any rate. Sounds more like a wake.'

The following day the Reverend Ian Hazelwood arrived at the main door at 8.30am clutching a small travelling case containing a silver platter and cup, as the Prince frequently liked to celebrate Communion in the privacy of his own home. Charles was the only one who made it to the service, and afterwards had a full English breakfast with the minister in the dining room. Diana chose to have a long lie-in, with the boys at her side.

She, the boys, Edward and Georgie all departed that afternoon while Charles stayed on for meetings. There was a miserable atmosphere. Charles and Diana could barely bring themselves to kiss each other as she walked through the back door and stepped into her car. Things looked so bad that none of us was really sure if they would be sharing many more weekends at Highgrove again.

And then, with perfect timing, Jimmy Savile arrived. Rather like the Prince's other good friend Spike Milligan, Jimmy seemed able to get to the heart of Charles's problems within a matter of minutes. As he waited for the Prince he puffed on his cigar and sent great clouds of blue smoke into the air. He knew that smoking was officially frowned on in the house but just laughed it off, saying: 'Oh, the Boss won't mind. He knows how much I like my cigars.'

Strolling around in his tracksuit, with the laces of his training shoes left undone, Jimmy Savile was the most unlikely spiritual comforter for Charles that could be imagined. He would drive up in his enormous mobile home and leave it parked like some incongruous monster in the back yard.

'Ah, Jimmy,' laughed the Prince as Paul ushered him through to the drawing room. 'How nice of you to come.' The pair remained shut away together for over an hour.

The atmosphere of crisis rose yet a further notch when Mrs Shand Kydd arrived for a second weekend on November 21. Charles had originally planned to travel to Scotland that weekend, but cancelled his arrangements at the last minute. He, Diana and her mother stayed up talking late into the night as the boys slept upstairs in the nursery, unaware of the discussions below.

Charles and his mother-in-law seemed perfectly at ease in each other's company, and if anything he seemed to make an effort to show how normal and considerate he could be. However, as soon as she had gone, the Prince resumed his hedonistic lifestyle, hunting and travelling around the country.

On December 22 a grand ball was held for staff at Buckingham Palace. The doors opened in the historic main hall, and the Queen and her family walked slowly through. The Queen and the Princesses present looked stunning in their ballgowns and tiaras as they circulated and talked to individual members of staff.

Diana, unlike the others, seemed to have the common touch, giggling and blushing with staff as if she were one of them and not the Princess of Wales. I could see Charles watching her out of the corner of his eye as she went round the room. He looked on as she took the mother of one servant in her arms and kissed her expansively on the cheeks. Charles's expression was one of horror, mixed with fascination that any wife of his could behave so normally with ordinary people. The horror seemed to arise out of a fear that she had taken over from him as the most important and popular young royal . . . and there was nothing he could do about it.

1988

———

CHAPTER EIGHT

The Riding Instructor

I t was a Saturday morning in early January, and after her Christmas break the Princess was in terrific form. Her good friend and former flatmate Carolyn Bartholomew, godmother to Prince Harry, had just been shown in, to find the Princess, with no shoes on, running towards her. William and Harry followed close behind, dressed in their favourite army fatigues. Both were kissed and hugged warmly by Carolyn.

Turning to her friend, Diana said: 'Now before we get down to a good gossip, guess who else I have invited?' Carolyn looked momentarily blank. 'David Waterhouse. You know – the army boy, silly. He should be here just before lunch.'

Diana was at her most buoyant and excited. It appeared that the Christmas break at Sandringham shortly before had led to some dramatic New Year's resolutions. Top of the list appeared to be a new, cheerful attitude to life, and, with her mind made up, her good mood was very infectious. A new year, and perhaps a new Diana, I thought, as I went to do a last-minute check of the Green Room where Carolyn Bartholomew would be staying.

Major David Waterhouse arrived shortly before lunch in a silver Audi. William and Harry had obviously met him many times before, and were delighted at having the thickset, 'real life' soldier staying for the weekend. 'David', William explained to his brother, 'uses real guns and kills people.' 'I don't think so, William,' giggled Diana, as the group sat down to lunch in the sitting room.

Prince Charles was away for the weekend, having popped into Highgrove for a night alone the previous Thursday. Like Diana, he seemed more relaxed and contented than I had seen him for many months. He had slept in Diana's double bed, something he always did when she was not there, and had commented on how good the mattress was. 'It's so much harder than my bed,' he told me. 'The support is fantastic.' I held my tongue, but felt like saying that, if it was so good, why didn't he sleep there when his wife was at home as well.

Carolyn, who had been to school with Diana, was one of her closest friends, and the two of them seemed inseparable. David, who was obviously a very good friend, was someone Diana relied on and bounced ideas off. 'I've known David for years,' she would say with a smile when we said how charming her friends were. 'He's such a dear, dear friend. But I suppose I must find a wife for him one of these days.'

All of them congregated in the kitchen shortly before midday as William and Harry finished their riding lesson with the groom, Marion Cox. The Sunday morning kitchen session became a ritual as the boys grew older. Both would come in, out of breath, to find Diana putting out pieces of carrot and apple on the sideboard. Armed with a knife each, and under very close supervision, they would chop up the vegetables to feed to the guinea-pigs and rabbits. Then they would grab handfuls of sugar lumps and take them out to 'thank' the ponies for their rides.

We were not to see the Prince and Princess together again until February 12, when they returned from their tour of Australia. Reading the enormous amount of press coverage gave us all quite a shock, since the newspaper and TV reports were filled with images of the two of them dancing and laughing together at every opportunity.

'Something strange is going on here,' said Paddy one morning as he sat at the large kitchen table. 'They've obviously had a good speaking-to by someone, and been told to put on a good show.' Paul agreed, looking aghast at the daily pictures of a couple apparently so much in love. But he added, 'Well, maybe something has changed between them. One thing is for sure, we will know the truth when they get back.'

Their first weekend of the new year together was a revelation, and certainly everything seemed to be much calmer between them. They were still in separate rooms at night, but the tension and dark atmosphere of the previous year appeared to have lifted. The tone of voice used when they called each other 'darling' in front of staff seemed altogether sweeter and more genuine than in previous months, and as a result William and Harry behaved much better.

William was by now old enough to be aware of the rows and tensions in his parents' marriage. No amount of play-acting can ever fool a child. However, as he sat down to breakfast that February morning with Charles and Diana, he must have seen his parents as an altogether closer unit. Charles, who the previous year had sent his elder son back to the nursery for his breakfast after a series of particularly noisy and badly behaved mealtimes, now cooed softly as William 'the Wombat', as he dubbed him, accidentally spilt yoghurt over his chair. Diana looked anxiously across at her husband as William giggled at the mess, and was surprised and pleased at the change in him.

'They might still not have a lot in common,' said Paul as he filled up another coffee pot for them that morning, 'but I do think things might be a bit more peaceful from now on.'

The staff were quite overcome by the sense of domestic bliss, even if the Prince and Princess spent much of the day apart. Despite his heavy workload, Charles never prevented the boys from going into any of the rooms, and quite often seemed to welcome their intrusion if he was in the middle of some boring paperwork. When he needed absolute peace and quiet he would ask them to play outside for an hour, then promise them a game of Big Bad Wolf upstairs later on. This was one of the boys' favourite pastimes. It consisted of Charles standing in the middle of the day-nursery floor and trying to prevent them getting past him. Sometimes it got quite rough, with little William and Harry being hurled on to the large sofa at the side, although nobody ever got hurt, because of all the cushions. Invariably they were prevented from passing and, amid gales of laughter, were spent spinning on to the sofa.

'Look at the mess, Wendy,' said an exhausted Charles as the boys were being tucked up in bed. 'Come on, I'll give you a hand putting everything back in its place.'

. . .

It was just before dinner on Thursday March 10. At home in Formby, I was on the verge of taking a joint out of the oven when the telephone rang. It was Paul, the butler, at Highgrove.

'Wendy, thank God I have reached you,' he spluttered. 'There has been the most terrible accident in Switzerland. The boss and the Princess are fine, thank goodness, but Major Hugh Lindsay, you know, the equerry, is dead. You had better get back here as soon as you can.' I turned on the evening news and, to my horror, saw pictures of the avalanche that had come so close to taking the Prince's life.

Only two days previously Charles and Diana had flown off to Klosters with a group of friends including the Duchess of York. Both had seemed relaxed and very much looking forward to the break. Then, on the Thursday, disaster struck. Although Diana and Sarah, who was pregnant at the time, had been resting in their chalet, Charles, his friends Mr and Mrs Palmer-Tomkinson, Hugh Lindsay and a ski-guide, Bruno Sprecher, were caught up in the avalanche. And when the snow and boulders had passed Major Lindsay was dead and Mrs Patti Palmer-Tomkinson badly injured.

I knew practically everyone in the group, and felt a great wave of shock come over me. It had been so close. The accident could so very nearly have changed the entire course of history, leaving young William and Harry without a father. I hastily gave my children some supper, then jumped in my car to make the four-hour drive back to Highgrove.

The Prince returned to the house on Saturday. Diana had chosen to go back to Kensington Palace with Sarah and Hugh Lindsay's widow. Dressed in black, Charles walked through to the sitting room. His face was ashen, and he looked as if he had not slept for days.

'I am so terribly sorry, Sir,' I said as he walked up to greet me.

'It has been the most terrible few days, I am afraid, Wendy,' he replied. 'Simply ghastly.'

That weekend, as arrangements were made for Hugh Lindsay's funeral, Charles seemed to be suspended in a state of shock. There were numerous phone calls from the Queen, Prince Andrew and Prince Edward. Charles took them all in his study, and wrote letters of sympathy to Hugh's family and widow.

'He's blaming himself for what happened, you know,' said Paul that evening after he had taken in a light supper tray, hardly any of which was touched. 'He is sitting there watching television with a completely blank look on his face. It's as if he can't comprehend quite what has happened.'

Diana obviously felt her place was in London, near Sarah Lindsay and Fergie. However, we considered her non-appearance at Highgrove sadly indicative of how little the couple shared, even at times of grief. Despite his stiff upper lip, Charles appeared at times on the verge of breaking down in tears. I think the realisation of how close he had been to death affected him far more than he acknowledged. But there was nobody there to comfort him and talk things over apart from his detectives and staff, whom he would not usually have burdened with such private matters. As he went up to his room that evening I saw a very lonely man climbing the stairs. His family, devoted to duty, carried on with their public engagements; Diana was in London with William and Harry; but Charles was at Highgrove, alone.

It was as if the avalanche and its tragic results had wiped out much of the newfound goodwill between Diana and her husband. Both the Prince and Princess needed people to help them grieve and come to terms with the loss, yet neither could turn to the other. The tragedy affected the rest of their lives, in several ways, since it appeared to spell the end of any mutual support.

Charles and Diana seemed to reach a truce of equal indifference that summer. No longer were there the bitter rows and recriminations of earlier years, but neither were there the spontaneous attempts to make up. In the past, a particularly nasty scene might have been followed by an attempted reconciliation. But now, neither seemed the slightest bit interested in what the other was doing. In front of the boys they were civil and polite, but when the children were in bed, there was practically no communication whatsoever.

Diana had given up her quest for a tennis court, but had miraculously found another pastime to fill her spare moments. And it was a hobby that took us all, including Paddy, by surprise. She had seen how much William and Harry enjoyed their pony rides, and suddenly announced that she intended to take up riding herself.

Paddy's reaction had been suitably scathing. After the initial shock of hearing her express an interest in something he considered exclusively to be the 'Prince and his sort's' interest, he remarked, 'It won't last. She's too bloody weak and timid to be able to handle a horse. I give her a month and then she'll give up.' However, he was wrong.

Above: James Berry
and three other
footmen in state livery
just minutes before a
royal banquet.

Above: The back door
t Highgrove – scene
f many a tearful exit
y Diana.

Right: Paddy
Whiteland, Charles'
right-hand man and
male confidant at
Highgrove.

Top: Highgrove's library – the round table piled high with books serves as Charles' desk. We were under strict orders never to rearrange the papers and books on the floor.

Above: The Sundial Garden, where Charles had breakfast on sunny mornings, which is overlooked by Highgrove's drawing-room.

Above: The Royal bath tub and shower, used at least twice a day by Prince Charles.

Left: Prince Charles' dressing-room – his bedroom, too, when Diana was in residence.

Above: Typical end to one of Diana's summer parties (left to right): me, Prince Harry, Ken Wharfe, Jessie Webb, Maria Burrell. Tigger's puppy Roo, since lost at Balmoral, in the background.

Above: Prince Harry helping to blow out the candles on my birthday cake, outside in Highgrove's garden in July 1992.

Above: Inside the drawing-room, totally redecorated after the separation of Charles and Diana.

Above: Highgrove's kitchen, where the chefs worked, and where Diana chatted way to the staff.

Right: At the kitchen sink.

Left: Me as Cruella de Vil receiving my prize from Diana at Maria Burrell's fancy-dress birthday party.

Below: Diana's chef Mervyn Wycherley, body-builder and pizza-maker extraordinaire.

Above: Butlers at play. Paul Burrell, left, former butler at Highgrove, and Harold Brown, right, his counterpart at Kensington Palace, off duty.

Right: Into the real world – my farewell lunch at one of Diana's favourite London restaurants, San Lorenzo, in early summer 1993.

Above: Diana at the christening of the twin sons of Fay Appleby, her former dresser.

Left: Maria Burrell, until recently Diana's dresser and a former housemaid at Highgrove, with James the gardener at a Christmas staff get-together in a local pub near Tetbury.

Above: The Lodge by Highgrove's front gates – my home for eight years.

Above: Perk of the job – tickets to Ascot. My son James Berry and I with Palace footman Keith McGloire.

Above: James Berry in livery stepping up on to a royal carriage at Ascot.

Right: 'Come on you blues!' The Queen and Zara Phillips at an informal football match at Windsor Castle.

Even though she never did any riding at Highgrove, she would stop off on her way down to ride out with a new friend who was also teaching the boys. The new riding instructor had obviously made quite an impression on Diana, who would chat away happily to the boys about their trotting and cantering and how much they had improved. He was a handsome, copper-haired cavalry officer called James Hewitt. With his perfect manners and easy-going charm, he seemed to be ideal for the young princes. They liked him so much that before long they were asking if he could come and stay at weekends. Diana readily agreed, betraying a warmth and depth of affection between her and the riding instructor that surprised everyone.

James's visits were at first sporadic, and he would arrive for the odd night when the Prince was away. He joined in happily with the staff's routine, and could often be found chatting with William and Harry in the kitchen as they cut up the food for the rabbits and fed the goldfish.

The air of relaxed domesticity between Diana and James should have set alarm bells ringing to anyone with their interests at heart. It was obvious that a mutual infatuation was taking them in a very dangerous direction. 'Oh, James, you are spoiling them rotten,' she giggled as he handed round the tin of 'royal' biscuits to the staff in the kitchen. 'Come on outside for a walk, and let them get on with the lunch.' We watched with concern as Diana led him out and on to the terrace, her face coloured and excited by his visit.

'So Diana's got her own special friend now, just like the Prince,' chuckled Chris Barber, one of the chefs. 'I suppose it could only have been expected.'

I grew bothered by the frequency of James's visits and dreaded the Prince's asking me a direct question about him. I would not know what to say. I thought Diana could not be keeping the visits a secret, because of the boys being there. They were bound to have mentioned him. For the moment I decided I would treat the whole matter as a gentle infatuation, at least until there was evidence to the contrary. It would be another twelve months before that was to happen.

That summer Charles threw himself into his polo with a vigour and passion that surprised even Paddy. 'He's pushing himself too hard,' he said one day. 'It's as if he feels under pressure to prove his riding skills. I don't know what has got into the man...' But we did. He was discovering how close his wife was growing to the other polo star in her life, Major James Hewitt, and did not like the air of competition one bit.

Meanwhile Charles's nocturnal visits to Camilla continued as before, with the Prince snatching as much time as possible with the Brigadier's wife. The Prince would often drive a staff car when visiting Camilla and other friends in the area, and rarely his Aston Martin. Arrangements and dinner dates were hurriedly cancelled and rearranged at the last minute; the Royal Train, originally booked for departure at 11pm, was changed to 2am on the morning of June 2.

'Why does he want the train so late?' I innocently asked when told of the change of plan. 'He wants to go out for dinner,' said Paul. 'And he's going to be out for some time.'

. . .

It was Diana's twenty-seventh birthday, and Highgrove was overflowing with staff and children. Diana, Ev and Ruth Wallace, the nanny, all arrived in high spirits on the Friday afternoon, and the boys headed straight for the swimming pool. Diana, looking radiant in cotton trousers and a flowered top, rushed into the house with carrier bags full of presents. I had put a wonderful bunch of tulips in her room, and she thanked me for them and the card I had sent to Kensington Palace the day before. It was going to be a relaxed family weekend, she said, and she had arranged for William and Harry to have Ella, Prince and Princess Michael's daughter, little Gabriella Kent, whom she adored, to play with.

That night, Charles returned with Colin Trimming, his detective, from an engagement in Scotland for a special birthday dinner prepared by Enrico, their charismatic new Italian pasta chef. He had quickly discovered the Prince's likes and dislikes and introduced him to the idea of having crudités before a meal with a mayonnaise or tomato dip. There was also Parma ham cut from sides stored in the pantry. Charles grew so fond of this dish that he went completely overboard, and asked for it before every dinner. On days when it was late appearing we would get a call in the pantry, with Charles saying in a mock-angry growl: 'Where's the bloody crudités?', the joke on the word *crudité* amusing him no end.

The birthday supper that night was quiet and civilised, with both Charles and Diana retiring early to bed, and to their separate rooms. Diana took some late-night phone calls from friends, but was asleep by midnight. She had said from the start that she did not want a fuss made, and Charles had gone along with her wishes. 'I get so exhausted, Wendy,' she explained early the next day. 'I can barely keep my eyes open after 10pm.'

With Charles due to play polo, Diana, Ella, William and Harry went off to visit Bowood House, owned by one of the Prince's close friends, the Earl of Shelbourne. It was later said to be a secret meeting place for Charles and Camilla. Diana, however, seemed oblivious to the house's significance, and looked upon the visit as a treat for the children. Unfortunately there was an accident – Ella fell from a climbing frame and broke her collar-bone. She was suffering from concussion and had to be rushed to hospital. Ruth, who had been Ella's nanny before working for the Prince and Princess, went to hospital with her, staying the night to comfort the frightened little girl. This meant that Ev and I had to look after Harry the following day while Diana took William to polo.

Harry was most miffed about not being able to see his father play. Diana looked at me exasperatedly. 'You know the problems, don't you, Wendy? The place will be overrun with press, and without Ruth to keep control the boys could start a riot. That's the last thing I need at the moment.' She added quietly to her younger son, 'Don't worry, darling. Let's ask James to teach you about polo the next time we see him.' Harry looked up and smiled, mirroring the expression on his mother's face.

CHAPTER NINE

The Dog and Duchess

A heavily pregnant redhead stood puffing and out of breath at the front door, her cheeks covered in beads of sweat. 'Hiya,' boomed Fergie, brushing past Paul and walking into the sitting room. 'Is the Prince around?' Behind her walked her lady-in-waiting, Helen Hughes, her head slightly bowed as she struggled under the weight of several overnight bags.

Unlike her friendship with Diana, which was beginning to cool, Sarah's relationship with Charles seemed to be growing closer by the week. She would ring up and ask his advice on the most trifling of things, ranging from polo matters to which charities she should try to become involved with.

'Get us some tea, will you?' she asked of no one in particular when told the Prince was due back at 6pm. 'Helen and I are gasping for a cup.' Paul and I exchanged worried glances. We were both envisaging a busy stay.

Since her marriage to Andrew, Sarah Ferguson had changed no end, from a rather frumpy Sloane into a very demanding young madam. I looked at her brand new, smart, very expensive luggage and smiled at the contrast with the battered old plastic suitcases she had had before her marriage. She was obviously loving every moment of her newfound importance as a Duchess, and was going to be a stickler for detail.

'That woman,' said Paul through gritted teeth as we narrowly missed kicking Bendicks, Sarah's dog, on our way through to the kitchen to prepare the tea tray.

When Charles arrived he rushed through to greet them, showing a genuine warmth and humour rarely bestowed on his wife. 'Charles,' shrieked Sarah, as he walked through the door. 'How brilliant to see you.' That evening the Prince, the Duchess and her lady-in-waiting all ate together in the sitting room. Diana was away and not due for another 48 hours. The sound of laughter rang through Highgrove. Though heavily pregnant with her elder daughter, Beatrice, Sarah was still in fine form, and cracking raucous jokes at everyone's expense until well past 11pm.

I was expected to take up the early morning tray and pack the Duchess's things the following day. As I walked along the landing I could hear the sound of barking and giggling from her room. Knocking gently, I walked in and was confronted with one of the most preposterous sights I have ever seen. Lying on her back like a beached whale, and with her nightdress up around her breasts, the Duchess of York was balancing Bendicks on her massively swollen belly. With only a month to go before the birth, Fergie's tummy was huge, an almost impossible mountain for Bendicks to climb. As I walked in she was balancing the dog on top of her and roaring with laughter, the terrier yapping and barking as she pulled at its legs to keep it in position.

'Oh, good morning,' she blushed violently, tossing Bendicks to one side and pulling the sheets over her as she heard me come in. 'Just put it down on the side there, please.' I looked at her case and asked if she wanted me to press anything. 'Oh, I shouldn't think so,' she said initially, but then changed her mind: 'Oh, come to think of it. Give it all the once-over, will you.'

I stared in horror at the two bags filled with blouses and maternity clothes. 'All of it, Ma'm?' I responded. 'Yes,' she said firmly, 'all of it.'

. . .

Fergie, by now dressed in an exquisitely ironed maternity suit, spoke quietly and confidentially with the Prince for a few minutes before joining Helen in the car. 'It'll be all right. I know it will, Charles,' she said softly as they stood alone together. 'These things just take time.'

Then, with a kiss, and a curt 'Bye' to Paul and me, she waddled to the car and drove away.

The next day Diana arrived very late, with no nanny or dresser. Charles had already gone to bed and was up and off to polo before Diana surfaced at breakfast. Neither spoke to the other that weekend, since Harry and his mother were in bed whenever Charles eventually returned. On Sunday Diana went back to London in tears, her face hidden by a baseball cap brim. Dashing out through the back door, she was so upset she could not even say goodbye.

I looked at Paul and wondered what on earth had happened to cause such a scene. Diana's phone had gone non-stop during her stay, but there had not been any of the usual rows or niggles. 'Problems in London?' suggested Paul. 'No doubt we'll find out sooner or later.'

The constant mood swings, which took Diana from delirious happiness to despair, were turning into an irritating and confusing pattern for all of the staff. None of us knew quite what to expect when she arrived for the weekend stop-overs, either with or without the nursery. So it came as no real surprise when, after months of tears and indifference, Charles and Diana arrived for their seventh wedding anniversary at Highgrove looking as happy as newlyweds. I had filled the rooms with cut flowers, and both the Prince and Princess seemed overwhelmed by their scents and colours. 'How romantic, Charles, look...' said Diana as she pointed to an enormous bunch of wild roses on the piano in the hall.

That weekend Charles and Diana and their sons sat together at meal-times, and relaxed by the pool during the hot summer afternoons. They were a picture of domestic contentment, lounging around in swim-suits and towelling robes, and ringing through for jugs of lemon refresher. And, as always, their mood was infectious. Charles and Diana actually chased each other around the pool at one stage, both ending up falling in, to the delight of William and Harry.

The boys were due to stay with us for a week, and spent the days running around in shorts, swimming, riding and firing their water pistols at anyone who came within range. Both were brimming with excitement about their holiday in Majorca and spent hours discussing what they were going to do there when they arrived.

. . . .

With the royals away most of the summer, either in Spain or up in

Scotland, Paul and I set about giving Highgrove its annual clean. As in previous years, it was Charles who made brief overnight stays to check on the operation, taking a delight in even the most minor alterations and subtle changes of paint.

New mobile telephones were delivered from the Palace, along with instructions that, in the light of the various taped conversation scandals, now seem extremely ironic. Although we were told they were more expensive to use than land lines, the real concern appeared to be over security. One memo underlined the risk, pointing out, 'Speech on mobile phones is not just insecure; it is very easy to intercept.' Of course, none of us quite knew how easy, until tapes of the Prince's and Princess's intimate conversations were published in the newspapers.

As autumn approached there were more visitors to Highgrove, including Diana's mother Frances Shand Kydd, Sarah Lindsay with her baby, Alice, and Princess Beatrice with her nanny. Diana was absolutely bowled over by her niece and took William and Harry up to see her. She was at her most natural with young babies, and flushed excitedly as she held the tiny child in her arms. She fussed over little Alice, too, as if she was never going to drag herself away from the child.

There was an unspoken bond between Diana and Mrs Lindsay following the avalanche: no matter what happened she or Charles would always look after her. Sarah Lindsay herself was remarkably calm and composed, taking solace in the fact that Hugh's baby was alive and well even if Hugh was not there himself.

Bruno Sprecher, the friend of Fergie's who had acted as ski-guide that day, also spent an October weekend with Charles and Diana. He turned up looking extremely dapper in a sharp jacket and jeans, his beard neatly trimmed along tidy geometric lines. Charles and Diana later explained they felt it important that he come over and stay in case he blamed himself for the accident. Both the Prince and Princess were polite and welcoming to him, but there didn't appear to be the same depth of friendship between them and the ski-guide as between him and Fergie.

Fergie's nanny, Alison Wardley, who turned up in a mini-skirt, was much younger than I had expected, and was extremely open and friendly with the staff. Everyone was interested in finding out what life was like with the Duchess, and some of those who had worked at Buckingham Palace with Andrew wanted to know if he had changed. Alison expertly fielded the personal questions, but her observation that

Fergie 'could be really quite difficult, like anyone,' appeared to be the tip of the iceberg.

After the problems of previous years Diana seemed resigned to the differences between her and Charles's characters, and more in control of her emotions. She appeared more mature and confident than I had ever seen her before, and single-minded about what she wanted out of life. They did not sleep together, at least not at Highgrove, but seemed to have come to terms with their lot. The strange thing was that we knew Charles was still visiting Camilla, although by this stage she did not come so frequently to Highgrove, and Diana was spending a lot of time with her friend James Hewitt. But tempers and emotions had cooled enough in their marriage to allow a balance, and consequently a calmer atmosphere at home.

. . .

The weather had now turned and Charles, dressed in cords and an old heavy woollen sweater, sat alone at breakfast. It was November 14 and he had woken up to the realisation that he was forty years old. A neat pile of presents had been laid out on the table by his valet. Among the small packages and cards was a little box – Phyllosan tablets, from the police post outside. Inside the box was a jokey card, suggesting they might come in useful now he was heading towards old age. The Prince laughed, but looked more depressed than for several months. He had the air of a deeply sad man, whose youth had somehow slipped past without his realising it. 'Does it hit everyone a bit like this?' he asked Ken, the valet, that morning. 'I didn't expect it to be quite so bad.'

As if to make matters worse, Diana came downstairs at her most playful. 'Morning, darling. What does it feel like to be old?' she joked.

The main Christmas staff ball that year was at Buckingham Palace, and I had arranged for an old friend to come with me. As Joe Loss and his orchestra struck up the first dance, Prince Philip approached a lady member of staff and asked for a dance. Fergie was there with Prince Andrew, and I noticed she was coming in our direction, a broad grin on her face. As she bounced up to us I began to introduce my guest. A look of confusion furrowed her brow. 'Well, who on earth are you?' she barked, somewhat officiously. I explained I had looked after her at Highgrove. 'Oh yes,' she replied aloofly, 'so you did', and walked away.

I was not angry so much for myself as for my guest. 'Are they always that rude?' he asked me. 'Your life must be made a misery.'

1989

CHAPTER TEN

Staff Confidences

Evelyn Dagley, Diana's dresser, tapped on the Princess's bedroom door and walked in with the early morning tray. Pulling back the curtains, she said good morning and went through to the bathroom to run Diana's bath. The Princess sat bolt upright in bed and looked around her, rubbing the sleep from her eyes.

'God, Evelyn,' she shouted. 'What on earth have you been eating? You absolutely stink of curry. Get out and wash your hair, will you. I can't stand that smell,' she bawled as she jumped out of bed and made for the bathroom. 'Yuk, it's revolting.'

I came across Ev in tears and was told about the curry drama. Ev explained that she had got up at 5am to bathe and wash her hair after having a curry the night before with friends. 'I know she doesn't like the smell of garlic or curry powder and so I was reluctant to have it in the first place,' she sobbed. 'But this is just so personal and unfair.'

All I could smell was soap and shampoo and I told her so. 'It's just what I thought,' said Evelyn sadly. 'There's no reason why she should have shouted at me like that apart from the fact that she has woken up, once again, in a particularly foul mood.'

Palace guidelines for royals and staff about what they could and could not eat were very strict. All of us were advised to avoid garlic and strong spices for fear of offending the delicate noses of visiting VIPs and other royals. As far as I was concerned the odd piece of garlic never really revealed itself, but Diana, whose sense of smell seemed second to none, was always on the look-out.

I was beginning to understand the strain Ev was under. She was such a carefree and happy character in the early days, and would do anything asked of her. But as the Prince and Princess continued to fight and grow apart, Diana appeared to transfer all her worries and tensions on to the staff immediately around her. The dresser's position is one of the most intimate in the household, and therefore potentially the most dangerous, being at the cutting edge.

I would often find Evelyn, who was by no means a little mouse, close to tears as she sat slumped on her bed. I would try to comfort her as her dark eyes filled with tears while she recounted yet more unreasonable demands from her boss. It appeared that the more efficient and hard-working she was, the more Diana criticised her. If the towels were expertly folded and the clothes packed immaculately in tissue paper, Diana would point to her shoes and say they hadn't been polished well enough.

'I really don't know what to do at times,' said Ev despairingly that morning. 'I sometimes think it would be better for me just to resign and get out. After all, that is all she really wants me to do, isn't it?'

.   .   .

William and Harry were growing up into super young boys. When Diana had one of her moods the quickest way through would be for her to take them out for some shopping or a visit to a local fair, and we all hoped for this. The Princess was turning increasingly towards her elder son for a real sense of companionship, and though she loved both boys equally, one could sense the strong bond between her and William.

The sound of laughter filled the back yard. William and Harry raced up the back steps through the staff area and into the hall. Diana chased after them, followed by the detectives, Dave Sharp and Ken Wharfe. It was early February and neither Diana nor the boys had been to the house at all since Christmas, spending the first few weeks of the year at Sandringham with the Queen or in London.

'Hello, everyone,' shouted Diana as she ran past. 'A belated but very Happy New Year.'

Charles was away, and Diana was light-hearted and cheerful. All were out of breath as they sat around the kitchen table, the boys digging into a tin of Benoist biscuits, and Diana and Ken discussing the performance of Verdi's *Requiem* they had both attended the night before. To everyone's delight, Ken got up from the table, grabbed a biscuit from the tin, and serenaded it in a rich baritone voice. William and Harry looked up in amazement. Diana collapsed into a fit of giggles. She found her ruddy-complexioned detective hysterically funny, and clapped and cheered when he had finished singing, encouraging him to break into a song and dance routine around the table. He tapped and pirouetted his way around the kitchen, lapping up the attention and clutching hold of my shoulders as he passed me. 'Oh, Wendy,' he serenaded me, 'Sole mio...'

Diana looked well and happy. The mood swings appeared to have gone and she seemed in total control.

That weekend William and Harry joined their mother for lunches and dinners in the sitting room in front of the TV. It was a treat for them all since Charles, when there, would sometimes grumble about how much time they spent watching the box. On the Saturday evening I went in with some apple juice for the boys to find Diana sitting on the sofa, one son on either side of her, deeply engrossed in a TV film. The boys nestled against her in their pyjamas and dressing gowns. Diana looked totally relaxed. She had kicked her shoes off and tucked her legs under her, hugging both children as they sat and watched the film.

'Oh, Wendy,' she laughed. 'It's so frightening. Thank goodness I have my two strong men with me.' She looked ecstatically happy, as did William and Harry.

The phone rang. 'It's Papa,' said Diana, as she handed the receiver first to William and then to Harry. Both chatted away to their father on the other side of the world, telling him about their riding that day and what they had been up to at school. The conversation went on for more than ten minutes before Diana was put back on the line.

'Yeah, I'm absolutely fine,' she said quietly. 'Hope you're having a good time.' She looked wistful as her husband recounted a minor detail about the visit to her. 'Well, you are very lucky to be somewhere hot,' she said sadly. 'Goodnight then...' She put the receiver back and tried to get back into the film. But her mind was elsewhere.

. . .

'I really don't know how you can go back there, Charles. Are you listening to me?' Diana's words rang through from the garden to the pantry. Charles, on his knees, was busy digging a patch of soil with a small trowel. His wife stood over him, dressed in cords and a waxed jacket, berating him as he stoically continued digging.

'Good God, man, it only happened last year,' she shouted. 'Have you forgotten already? Have you forgotten what happened there?' Poor Diana was fighting a losing battle over the Prince's planned visit to Klosters the following day.

'What will Sarah think? What will everyone think? How could you be so uncaring and insensitive, Charles?' she continued shouting. 'You know, sometimes I really don't think you have any comprehension about people's feelings.'

Charles looked up slowly from the plot of earth and said quietly: 'Diana. I am going and that is the end of it. I need to go back to prove, if nothing else, that I haven't lost my nerve there.' He added, getting up, 'Now if you'll excuse me I've got to go and see what is being packed for the trip.'

Diana was visibly upset as she read reports of his skiing holiday, refusing to speak to her husband when he rang through for Harry in the evenings.

'It's the same as it always is,' said one of the policemen in the staff sitting room that evening. 'He does exactly what he wants to do, even if the world and his wife are against it.'

'Not his fault entirely,' I replied.

'No, you're right,' he responded. 'It's the system. It's always the bloody system to blame.'

. . .

The atmosphere between Charles and Diana was lugubrious and strained the next time they were together at Highgrove, and had it not been for the arrival of Sir David Frost's three boys, Miles, Wilfred and George, it could easily have exploded into fireworks.

Diana assiduously kept apart from her husband, having still not forgiven him for the week in Klosters. She threw herself into entertaining the youngsters while Charles worked in his study, joining the rest of the party only for lunch and supper. Diana had a soft spot for the

Frost boys and kept a picture of the three of them in a wooden frame on her mantelpiece.

It was Charles and Diana's last weekend with the boys before an official visit to the United Arab Emirates and Kuwait. Charles would always be more nervous before a joint foreign trip than a solo visit, and that Saturday was no exception. His mind seemed elsewhere as he asked Wilfred Frost about school and what projects he was involved in. I used to smile at the way he treated young boys as fully fledged, intelligent adults, and it often brought out the best in them. His manner was a contrast to Diana's sense of fun and playfulness. She tended to be stricter about other things, such as eating sweets, which she tried unsuccessfully to ban on several occasions.

Although she dressed herself in the most luxurious and expensive fashions, Diana had a strong grasp on the cost of small things – or at least professed to have in front of her staff. She would get terribly annoyed when stories appeared in the papers claiming she had blown hundreds of thousands of pounds on herself over the years. 'People just don't understand what I have to put up with,' she moaned one afternoon. 'What am I expected to do? Walk around in a frumpy dress all the time? Then what would happen? I would be criticised for that as well.'

Despite her recent public aversion to luxury and exotic new clothes, Diana loved to be pampered. She evinced real excitement at having flown back from the Middle East in a private jet.

'It was just like being in some James Bond film,' she explained, her eyes wide open and sparkling. 'It wasn't that big, but it was so luxurious. We could order practically anything we liked. I really don't know why we don't get one. They are so much smaller and easier to manage than the big planes in the Queen's Flight. But I know what the Prince will say. *He* won't even get me a tennis court.'

The Princess was growing increasingly close to certain members of staff, something she did continuously over the years. It was an unenviable position for anyone to be in, because however close you became to her you always knew that eventually she would change her mind about you and move on to the next person. It was a very manipulative and calculated way to keep people on their toes, since it instilled absolute devotion in the lucky few 'chosen' for special treatment, for fear of being dropped.

Her style of confiding in the staff concerned Charles, who, though considerate and kind, would never treat us as friends, because of the unspoken barrier in his mind betwen staff and employers. Charles felt intrinsically that it was not a good idea for the boys to become too close to the Burrells' two children, for instance, because of the social gulf between them. Diana dismissed his reservations as 'old-fashioned nonsense' and 'behind the times'. I, however, could understand his misgivings. After all, Paul was his butler and Maria a former housemaid.

'The boys are Princes and should be reared as such,' said Charles rather pompously one evening to Diana in the sitting room.

'They may be Princes but they are my children as well,' snapped Diana. 'And they need to have a normal life or they will end up as hopelessly out of touch as you are.' With that she flounced off to bed.

Diana either could not or would not understand the conflict of loyalties, and she is lucky that William, who is fussed over more than any other boy his age, can cope so well. Much of that sense of responsibility appears to have been instilled in him just as much by his father as by his mother, however, and people do tend to forget that.

· · ·

Both William and Harry adored outdoor life, and were happy pottering around the farm, watching the lambing and learning to understand nature's cycle. Neither was squeamish about dead animals; William in particular found a morbid fascination in the rabbits and other creatures that Tigger caught. They were also aware of other brutal sides to country life. There was the magpie trap, for example. This contraption was designed to lure the birds and catch them so that they could be destroyed later. William and Harry seemed totally unbothered by it, peering eagerly at the frightened birds waiting for death inside. I was unhappy about the trap but didn't let on – I knew my misgivings would be dismissed as the whingeing of a soft townie. It did cross my mind to release the birds secretly, even if they were considered pests, but I didn't dare.

Charles felt intense joy that his sons should understand and care about country life, and was hurt, albeit at first without acknowledging the fact, that he began to acquire a reputation in the press for being a selfish and remote father.

Unlike Diana, who knew exactly what the game was, he did not understand why he was getting such bad coverage, and there were many occasions when I wished I could have taken him to one side and pointed out that there was a media battle being waged by his wife right under his nose. Such a thing would have been impossible for me to suggest, of course, but I always felt that some of his close friends, or perhaps Palace press officers, could have made him aware of certain tricks to encourage good publicity.

It is well known that Diana is more of a city dweller by nature than a lover of the countryside. This became patently obvious to us all when the boys wanted to go out for long walks. Diana would be the first to suggest doing something together, but would often return within a matter of half an hour to watch TV or listen to music rather than stay outside – especially when it was cold.

In April, Diana's sisters and their families descended on Highgrove. Prince Charles was away again in Scotland, which gave all three Spencer girls a chance to unwind. Neil McCorquodale, who had married Diana's sister and Charles's old flame Sarah, was a breath of fresh air, but Robert Fellowes, Jane's husband, was slightly more reserved and more of a born courtier. Dressed in country cords, he continued to wear a tie, and looked slightly uneasy out of the suit he usually wore. Nevertheless there was more noise and fun that weekend without the Prince than if he had been there, with all three families eating together in the dining room and running around the house.

'This is what this house should really be like,' said Paul as he sorted out the drinks tray that first Friday evening. Paul and Maria were by now basking in the close friendship of the Princess, who treated them as confidants. 'Highgrove is designed for big family gatherings like this, you know. Such a pity that the Prince is not always the one to appreciate that.'

In fact, Charles did make an unexpected visit on the Saturday, arriving by helicopter to spend the day with his wife and children. It could not be helped, but as soon as he arrived everyone moved into another, slightly more formal mode of behaviour. It was as if having the Princess of Wales there didn't make any difference, because she was part of the Spencer family, but Charles, as the genuine royal, was another matter.

For weeks the Princess had been complaining about her wisdom teeth and said she was going to have to have them removed. 'Everyone will say, no doubt, that I am having plastic surgery,' she said, 'but the truth will be my teeth, just in case you are asked.' She added, 'It's going to involve a general anaesthetic, but my mouth is just too overcrowded. Sounds dreadful, doesn't it?'

The Princess, who through watching *Casualty* seemed to have a working knowledge of most medical conditions, then talked about her nose. 'People are always saying I have had a nose job, which is ridiculous. Look at the bump on it, Wendy. I hate it but I promise you I've never had it touched.'

Pandemonium reigned in the house. Tigger had just had a litter of puppies and the Prince was deciding what to do with them all. In the end he justified keeping one, which he named Roo, and the other two were given away to friends.

What we didn't realise until several weeks later was that the Prince had given one of the puppies to Camilla Parker Bowles. The significance of the gift – the Prince was absolutely devoted to Tigger and allowed her to go anywhere with him – was not lost on anyone at Highgrove.

CHAPTER ELEVEN

Separate Lives

'Wasn't it dreadful,' exclaimed Diana, her eyes wide. 'I don't really want to think about it, it was so awful.' The Princess and I were sitting at the kitchen table at Highgrove discussing the Royal Gala in aid of the Prince's Trust at the London Palladium on April 19, 1989. Originally it had been billed in the official diary as a David Frost Spectacular, but we both decided it was spectacular in only one area: the way it dragged.

'I must say I thought it was never going to end,' added Diana. 'Thank God Kiri Te Kanawa only sang one number. Had she done an encore like so many of the others we would have been there all night.'

My son James and I had been given tickets for the stalls. Diana said she had seen us sitting there and had tried to wave discreetly at us. 'I'm afraid I did spend a lot of the time just looking around the theatre,' she chuckled, 'trying to pick out the faces of people I knew.'

Charles had also been bored rigid, I was told, but had persevered more than his wife, since the whole event was in aid of the Prince's Trust. The fact that it was one of her husband's charity evenings that had come in for public criticism was not lost on Diana, who in a rather barbed way told him, 'If you don't mind me saying so, darling, you really must get the basic timing of events like these sorted out. They do tend to go so much more smoothly if everything is kept to a minimum.' Charles had taken the jibe well on the surface, saying he thought the whole event was splendid but perhaps just a fraction too long.

The Prince had spent much of the year travelling between Birkhall, Windsor, Sandringham and Highgrove, but still found time for private weekend visits to Italy and elsewhere. This summer he was determined to play as much polo as possible. Charles's interest in the sport had originally been instilled by Prince Philip, but it had now taken an obsessive hold of him in a slightly unhealthy manner. He didn't have that much time to practise, so he threw himself into as many games as possible in order to keep his hand in.

In the weeks leading up to the start of the season, Major Ronald Ferguson made numerous phone calls to the Prince at Highgrove. The major, Sarah Ferguson's father, held a privileged position as the Prince of Wales's polo manager, and had unlimited access to him.

On days when the Prince felt he had played badly, he would return to Highgrove in a filthy temper, shouting and cursing at himself for being so out of practice. He might ring the Major on his mobile phone and they would go over the problems, trying to iron them out.

The Major, a handsome man with heavy, bushy eyebrows, was a regular visitor to court circles. He would often appear at Christmas lunches and balls, and highly valued his position within the royal set. My son James said he would never forget the day of the announcement of Sarah's engagement to Prince Andrew. James recalled how the Major 'hopped up and down on one leg in sheer happiness, chewing his fingers on one hand, and letting out shouts of joy'. Sarah had done the unbelievable and was marrying into the Royal Family – his cup was overflowing.

Charles and Diana were now expertly missing each other at Highgrove, often by a matter of just a few minutes. Diana might arrive with the nursery for a Saturday but leave on the Sunday immediately after lunch, sometimes as little as twenty minutes before the Prince pulled into the drive with his retainers. The cross-overs were sometimes farcically close, and on at least one occasion the two convoys of royal personage and accompanying staff must have passed each other on the road.

The Prince's affection for Tigger and her puppy Roo knew no bounds. Unlike Diana, who couldn't really stand the sight of the little

Jack Russell terriers, Charles wanted them with him all the time. In the mornings the dogs were allowed to run into his room and jump into bed with him. And as the Prince lay in bed, listening to either the Radio 4 *Today* programme or one of his 'talking book' cassettes, Tigger and Roo would snuggle up alongside him or burrow down the sheets to his feet. It meant, of course, that the Prince's sheets were always covered in dog hairs and occasionally were a bit smelly.

Tigger and Roo were, after all, trained hunting terriers who had the run of the farm. This training was oddly juxtaposed with a pampered lifestyle, in which they jumped into the royal bed and ate chicken specially prepared by a royal chef. Diana called them the 'wretched dogs' and pushed them out of the way, but Charles would have taken them anywhere in the world had he been able to. Long-distance journeys in Britain, especially involving the royal train, allowed them to travel with him. They could not, of course, accompany him on foreign visits.

If he couldn't hear the scratching of claws on the Highgrove floors as he walked around, he flew into a panic, demanding to know what had happened to them. On one occasion he actually asked if I had accidentally made the bed with Roo still in it. I could see that he wasn't joking, and had to go upstairs with him to check there wasn't a tell-tale dog-shaped bulge at the bottom of the bed. As we looked over the smooth, newly made surface I saw a small pool of urine on the bedspread.

'Oh, Wendy, look, she's widdled on my bed again,' laughed Charles. 'Thank goodness she's all right. She must have been here after you made the bed so can't be that far away.' Though a dog-lover myself, I was astonished at the Prince's reaction. There was none of the fastidious squeamishness that might have been expected, merely an earthy humour as I started to pull back the cover.

'What are you doing, Wendy?' he asked. 'Surely you are not going to change the cover, are you? There's some blotting paper and soda over there. Just give it a dab down. It will be fine.'

. . .

As the summer progressed Charles fell into a routine of polo followed by drinks and late dinner parties with friends. He was still in close touch with Camilla Parker Bowles, and tried to spend his Sunday nights with her. She rarely visited Highgrove at this stage, and made a point of never talking to staff if she did. This, of course, was to change significantly later on, but for the time being Camilla was keeping a low profile.

Charles's policemen were under strict instructions not to mention the visits to anyone, but it soon became obvious what the Prince was up to. I was always suspicious when the royal train was commissioned, because Charles liked to delay its departure to give him time for a quiet supper elsewhere before it left. More often than not his dinner companion would be Camilla, who under cover of darkness was able to spend discreet evenings with him before he joined the train at Kemble station.

With her husband otherwise engaged, Diana avoided him, rarely bothering even to keep in phone contact unless it was something to do with the boys. As in previous years, she kept in close touch with her own 'gang', which included Philip Dunne, David Waterhouse and James Hewitt. Diana felt comfortable with all these men, since they were of her generation and treated her like a normal human being rather than a royal superstar. She could flirt with them, and did, without risking a public admonishing from her husband, because he wasn't there.

In fact, the little time they were spending together was causing us all a great deal of concern. Both seemed driven by a desire to avoid each other, because of the friction between them when they did. The tension at Highgrove was almost palpable that May as Charles's valet packed up the Prince's things for a trip to Turkey. He was going 'with friends' and Diana was refusing to speak to him.

'Diana, darling, can we talk?' asked Charles through her bedroom door.

'There's nothing to say to you, is there?' was his wife's reply.

It was almost a relief when the Prince finally left for his holiday with Camilla Parker Bowles and her husband, because Diana came out of her room and joined in the day-to-day running of the house.

Such family disharmony was common throughout the rest of the year. It was becoming patently obvious to anyone who worked with or knew them that someone or something was going to have to give. Both had reached the point where neither was even prepared to make an effort. In public there were still joint appearances, but in private their marriage was exposed as the sham it really was, with separate meals and separate lives, at least when the children were not around.

Such was the mutual indifference, even loathing, that on Charles's return from Turkey he travelled straight to Cirencester for a game of polo, and only then on to Highgrove. Diana, who knew of his plans, made sure she had left by the time he finally returned. As he walked through the front door, still caked in sweat and thoroughly worn out from the match and the flight back, Charles asked me where the Princess was. I told him she had gone back to London. 'Oh. I had no idea,' was all he said. The couple had not spoken to each other for over a fortnight, and were simply dropping out of each other's lives.

Just as with any crisis-torn family, Charles and Diana tried to make more of an effort at putting on a united front when William was back for his half-term break. Diana took both boys off to the Scilly Islands and was joined by Charles, who was able to cycle and ride with his children in relative anonymity. Although it was a mere two-day break, Charles and Diana travelled out and back separately, with the Princess and the boys arriving a full eight hours before her husband.

'It's all been a bit fractious, I'm afraid,' said Ev as she discussed the holiday with me. 'Neither of them were prepared to make much of an effort together. In fact, it got a bit embarrassing at times how little notice they took of each other.' Evelyn looked worn out, and her dark eyes had rings under them. 'Some holiday,' she muttered before going up to her bedroom. 'I could do with a month to get over it.'

That Sunday Diana left for London to attend a concert at the Barbican. Once again she dashed out through the back door in tears. Charles did not come down and say goodbye either, which was unusual – normally he saw her off, however upset she might be. 'In tears again,' muttered Paddy as the Princess ran through the door and into her car. 'What on earth is wrong with the girl? It must drive him mad.'

I looked at the Princess as the car pulled away – her eyes were swollen and red. I couldn't help feeling sorry for her, this beautiful girl trapped in what the outside world saw as a fairytale marriage, but which was in reality a living nightmare. Ever mercurial in character and moods, it was impossible for her to explain her difficulties and fears to the Prince, who simply was not equipped to deal with such complex emotional problems. Even as a member of her household I found her sulks and tears difficult to cope with, because they took complete control of her. Led by her emotions, Diana was not only fragile and vulnerable at times like these but defensive as well, which meant that any attempt at comfort or support was rejected. What she seemed to be crying out for was real love and affection from the Prince, yet rejecting it when it was offered. There were many occasions in the past when he had tried to kiss her as she left and Diana had pulled her head away. The Prince had now given up trying.

Diana's friendship with Sarah Ferguson was at an all-time low, and Princess Anne was not someone she felt comfortable with. Quite simply, there was hardly anybody within the Royal Family that she could trust or rely on to understand her problems.

One exception, who became more of an ally than most, was Prince Edward, who came to Highgrove that June after Ascot week. There was a softness and sensitivity about him that appealed to Diana, and the rather gauche public image that he sometimes displays was not evident at all.

'Edward was shy, retiring and a good sort,' James told me when he was reminiscing about his time as Edward's valet. 'Rather like his mother, he was polite and very conscious of the effort being made by all the staff around him – but a little of the staff's campness and melo-dramatics had not helped his sense of humour. He was not having the most wonderful time at university, and the fiasco about the Marines, which he had decided he wanted to leave, had heightened his sense of vulnerability at a time when everything should really have been going very well for him.

'It was odd,' added James, 'how on the one hand Edward could be so placid and yet so apparently gauche on the other. He really didn't have an official role to play within the Royal Family. As far as I was concerned he was a normal, sensitive, handsome young man. The one certainty, however, was his reliance on others for emotional support.

'First there had been one of his detectives, whom he worshipped, followed a few years later by another footman-cum-valet. This man, who was also to become very close to Princess Diana and Princess Anne, is good-looking, dark-haired, and perfectly mannered, but a terrible flirt and gossip. His relationships with women are entirely platonic – that is not the case, however, with men. Edward and he had developed a close bond over the years. However, the details were not very reliable, and varied from day to day, according to how much whisky and soda the valet had drunk.'

I had known Edward sporadically for many years, and had come to know a great deal about the rather confused young Prince. Earnest, ill at ease when on public show, Edward is potentially one of the most charming members of the entire family. Diana felt protective towards him and called him 'darling' with seemingly more affection than she did her husband. In a funny way I always believed she considered him a victim of the Royal Family in the same way that she was, and took comfort from that conclusion.

James and other members of Edward's staff always maintained that there was no powerful homosexual drive to the Prince. 'He's a bit dramatic, but who wouldn't be,' laughed James soon after he had left the Household. 'After all, there are more old queens below stairs than there are above.' Despite the rather rigid constrictions of much of royal life, all members of the family would have been aware that they were surrounded effectively by a pink 'mafia' of homosexuals. It never ceased to amaze me that there were not more flare-ups and rows. 'People would be very surprised to see the characters employed by the royals,' chuckled James to me once. 'I suppose the best way of describing us would be as a mixed bag. It was always a fun crew... and we all got away with murder. In a way it was a bit like being part of some gang in your last year at prep school – with a lot of camping it up thrown in.

'The royals had a token black footman, who in fact was not really black at all but of mixed race, which was just about as far as the royals would go on that front. He was very handsome, and a prolific Lothario whose liaisons were the talk of the Palace and contantly needed to be hushed up. The complete opposite of him was the man who was caught soliciting in a lorry park and who grew marijuana in his apartment. There was a lot of sex – both gay and straight – among the staff, and the whole Palace appeared to survive on vast quantities of drink and cigarettes.

'Whatever the time it was always a good time for a drink – when I look back on it I don't know how any of us survived. As a consequence of people going around half-cut a lot of the time, accidents and horseplay tended to get a little out of hand. People did fall off roofs while trying to climb into bedrooms, beautiful china and silverware did get dropped and smashed, and fireworks were let off at inopportune moments. There was also the famous case of two footmen getting caught with a stick of dynamite, though no one ever got to the bottom of quite why they were carrying it. Like so many things it was the talk of the Palace, but hushed up enough to avoid it leaking out into the papers.'

One evening after an AIDS awareness meeting Diana returned to Highgrove and chatted with me about what she had learned. 'I know I shouldn't worry, but I do,' she said, looking concerned. 'I mean, what on earth is going to happen at the Palace if someone becomes infected?'

She looked across at me knowingly. 'As far as I can see, as soon as one goes down with it the rest are going to fall like flies. What a terrible thought.' Diana, whose friends included many gays, never took a moralistic line on the subject. She was, however, enough of a realist to know of the very real dangers of an AIDS epidemic at the Palace. 'Apart from all the suffering, can you imagine the headlines?' she said, clearly aghast at having even thought about it in the first place.

. . .

As the long hot summer continued, Charles increasingly invited his friends over to Highgrove for drinks and dinner. Rather than joining in, Diana would often go straight to bed or ask for a dinner tray.

The Palmer-Tompkinsons were old friends of Charles's from years before, and in turn were close to the Parker Bowleses. They were frequent dinner companions for the Prince, and after the initial shock when Diana first raced off to her room, grew to accept the situation. Geoffrey Kent, the smooth owner of the travel company Abercrombie and Kent, was also a regular supper companion, especially in the summer months, because he bankrolled Charles's polo team to the tune of over a quarter of a million pounds a year. His wife, an American heiress called Joric, older than her husband, simply adored the connection with Charles.

Both the Kents and the P-Ts, as they were known, would say hello as they were shown into Highgrove and ask us how we were. They had a civilised and stabilising effect on the Prince during these rocky years with Diana, and without them I do not know how he would have been able to cope.

In turn, Diana continued to invite over James Hewitt and friends such as Carolyn and William Bartholomew when Charles was not around. Unlike Diana, who would simply walk off to her room without saying hello to her husband's friends, Charles would never have dreamed of ignoring people. So for Diana to feel relaxed she had to wait until her husband was elsewhere. She managed to have the Bartholomews over while Charles was away that August on the cruise of the Western Isles aboard *Britannia*. Charles had originally asked if Diana had wanted to go with him, but was firmly told 'no'. 'Thank goodness I don't feel obliged to go any more,' said Diana after he had left. 'At least I can now have some time to myself.'

William had gone to Portugal with some friends at the start of the holiday, but was due up at Birkhall in August. Diana reluctantly agreed to spend some days there with her children, but looked unhappy at the prospect. 'It's all so regimented, there's no space,' she would complain to Evelyn. Another worry was how the boys would behave, since they were always spoiled rotten by the household when they went to stay with the Queen. William was growing out of the tantrums he used to throw when he couldn't get his own way, but still had an eye for the main chance. The nannies were usually under intense pressure at Balmoral and Sandringham, because they had to bring the boys down to earth after a day's constant attention and praise. It was their job to show William and Harry how to respond and behave calmly, without believing they could get away with everything.

Diana, who was very close and loyal to her dresser Fay Marshalsea, was overjoyed at the news of Fay's new and serious romance, and went out of her way to help her choose clothes and scarves from her wardrobe to wear on nights out with her boyfriend. Fay and the Princess were never happier than when talking about men and gossiping about who was going out with whom. It was a fun, normal side to Diana that was amusing as long as you weren't her target. Diana's ability to talk with staff was a double-edged sword, however, since one moment she would be chatting away at your level, the next complaining about some work that she considered shoddy and below standard. And her ability to catch people out was legendary, either by listening in to staff's unguarded conversations, or changing her plans, either deliberately or unintentionally.

One Sunday in September Diana was due to leave in the red helicopter. She climbed aboard, the staff standing by the main door to see her off. As soon as the royals departed there was usually time for a bit of a rest. Paul and I and the housemaids would take a few hours off, perhaps going home or popping into town for a bit of shopping. The long hours and relentless work meant that most of us simply wanted to go to bed for a little while, because fourteen- and fifteen-hour days were far from unusual. On this occasion I was just about to doze off when, to my horror, I heard the sound of the helicopter returning. As I raced up the drive I could see Paul and several other members of staff rushing back as well. Panting breathlessly, I ran into the kitchen, to hear that a technical fault had developed and it had been decided to take a car instead.

Diana paced up and down the hall, looking at her watch. Catching my eye and Paul's she said humorously, 'I see what you all get up to when I'm not here! So sorry to disturb your normal routine.' With that she was ushered into a car for the drive to the engagement. 'She's just tense about being late for the job,' said Paul. 'I'm glad she found it funny, though.'

The same buoyant good mood was in evidence when her sister Jane and her offspring made another visit to Highgrove. The house was filled with the sounds of noisy youngsters running to and fro, and Diana never looked happier than when she was cradling several children in her arms at any one time. It was as if she were losing herself in her own and other people's children, as if she were returning to what had made her happy before her marriage: life as a nursery-school teacher.

That October Diana invited her good friend Catherine Soames and her son Harry over for the weekend while Charles was away again in Scotland. Catherine, a tall, blonde Jardine Mathieson heiress, was married to Nicholas Soames MP, Sir Winston Churchill's grandson and former equerry to the Prince of Wales. The word was that Catherine's marriage was in trouble, and indeed she was soon to leave her ebullient Member of Parliament husband for a skier. Catherine returned alone the following weekend and was shut away with Diana in the Princess's sitting room for most of the time. Both Catherine and Diana relied heavily on each other in times of crisis, and could be seen walking slowly around the garden, dressed in long coats and rubber boots, as they quietly discussed their problems.

. . .

Charles, it appeared, had decided to make an effort. 'I thought you might all like to join us at the public firework display in Tetbury,' he announced casually to the assembled staff one cold winter afternoon. 'It's a public job, but it could be quite fun.' A small group of us climbed into the Land Rover Discovery: Paul, Maria and their two sons, the Princess, William and Harry and me. It was tremendous fun. We were not bothered by anyone as we walked around waiting for the display to start. 'Just like being a normal person again, Wendy,' said Diana as we found ourselves a good position.

The Prince wandered over to a hot-dog cart and gave the stall-holder the shock of his life when he ordered ten for the assembled party – although he did not eat one himself. There was also candy-floss for those who wanted it, all paid for by the PPO.

Suddenly the air was filled with the sound of bangs and thunder-flashes as the display began. Minutes later bright lights were flashing all around us. I looked about in panic, thinking a firework was exploding dangerously close. 'Bloody press,' shouted the PPO as he pushed Diana and the boys away from a small scrum of photographers towards the Discovery. Diana jumped into the back with William and Harry and I took the front seat.

The photographers must have been disappointed. The only picture they got showed an angry middle-aged woman – me – scowling out through the windscreen, furious at having a good evening ruined by the paparazzi.

1990

CHAPTER TWELVE

The Blue Room

It was going to be a busy January weekend after what appeared to have been a very rough Christmas. Diana and the boys had already spent a few days at Highgrove while Charles continued his Christmas break at Sandringham. Although he was away and Diana was with the boys, she seemed in a foul mood. Staff who had been with them during the break talked of incessant squabbling, otherwise practically no communication whatsoever.

It was with the utmost trepidation, therefore, that we viewed the prospect of a rare weekend later in the month with Charles and Diana together now that the boys were back at school. What made things worse was that guests were involved. As it turned out, though, things could not have gone much more smoothly.

The brewery owner Peter Greenall and his wife Clare arrived on the 26th and were put in the Green Room. All of us waited next day at the main door as one of Charles's favourite comedians, Spike Milligan, and his wife Sheila walked slowly up the single step and into the main porch.

Dinner was set for 8pm and Michael Fawcett, the valet, was in a panic. He had unpacked Spike's black tie and I had unpacked a formal evening gown for his wife: apparently no one had explained that the Prince and Princess rarely ate or dressed formally at Highgrove. Shortly after 7.30 Michael went through to the Prince to explain that he thought the Milligans were going to put on formal evening wear. Charles had no intention of making them feel ill at ease. In the end he himself walked up to the couple's room, to find Spike struggling with a starched collar and shirt. Guffaws of laughter could be heard as Charles explained there was no need to dress up for dinner, however good the food and service might be at his house. 'But you are the bloody Prince of Wales,' said Spike laughing. 'If I can't wear it with you, when can I wear it?'

In a pair of cords and a smart casual shirt, Charles welcomed them into the sitting room for pre-dinner drinks. Spike, in black tie, kept Charles, Diana and their guests in stitches for the rest of the evening. 'I must come here more often,' he said as he left the following day after lunch. 'It's been my best audience to date.'

A few weeks later Spike sent a small plaque to Highgrove, which he asked to be put up on the wall. It read 'Spike Milligan slept here', and was put on the Blue Room mantelpiece next to the enamel solar clock – a £45,000 wedding present!

Diana left soon after the Milligans, Charles later that evening. They seemed calmer and happier together of late, largely, we surmised, because they had been able to enjoy each other's friends. Unlike previous occasions, the Prince and Princess had presented a united front, eating and entertaining together. But it was not to last.

.   .   .

There were more staff changes in the pipeline. Within a few days we heard that Ruth Wallace, the nanny, had handed in her notice. The boys had grown extremely attached to her. She wasn't as formal as other nannies, and this put her on the right side of Diana, who liked her more relaxed attitude with William and Harry. Having come from the employ of Prince and Princess Michael of Kent, Ruth had simply had enough and wanted a change, but was asked not to tell the boys until Charles and Diana had found a replacement for her.

Diana was plunged back into a deep depression during the first few months of 1990, and seemed less able to cope with her husband's travelling, which was in fact no more frequent than in previous years. As he flew around Europe making environmental films, Diana took refuge with friends and their children. Both William and Harry were at school, and Diana missed them terribly. She hated the heartache and wrench their absence caused her, and invited her niece Beatrice over with some of her friends. Fergie had flown to New York again and Diana jumped at the opportunity of seeing more of Bea. 'I do love having children around me,' she explained one Sunday morning as I chatted to her in the sitting room. 'It gives life to a house.'

Half-term was eagerly looked forward to. With Charles away, Diana brought the boys to Highgrove and invited little Gabriella Kent to stay to keep them company. It was quite obvious that Diana desperately wanted more children. She looked so affectionately at Bea and Ella that your heart almost broke for her. I was sure, then, that had Charles agreed to try for more children, everything might have been saved in their strained marriage.

All too quickly the boys' half-term break was over, and Diana was faced with the prospect of trying to fill her time with things that interested her and kept her motivated. Charles was off to Switzerland. Diana, who had engagements at home, was not travelling with him, and clearly could not face the prospect of a long stay under the same roof with her husband.

Like several other members of staff I was becoming increasingly worried about the ultimate end of their feud. When a flash flood in Wales forced the Prince to break off his skiing and join his wife to inspect the damage, we all noticed how sad and distant they appeared in each other's company. It looked as if they were locked in some sort of living hell together, and I remember agreeing with Paul that the marriage was in a final stage of free fall.

As soon as Charles had completed his inspection of the flood-ravaged area he returned to Highgrove for a solitary supper rather than join his wife in London. He ate alone in his study, a meal that had been especially driven up from London by Michael Fawcett. It was as if the house had recently suffered a bereavement. Charles's gloomy mood spread to every corner of the building, the atmosphere only lifting when he returned to Switzerland the following day.

I was not to see Diana again until late April, when she turned up unexpectedly with the boys but no nanny. I was told to prepare for three guests that weekend, one of whom was James Hewitt. Nothing had been arranged in advance and none of her friends signed the visitors' book. Chris Barber, the chef, was on duty, however, and as

William and Harry were staying with her I presumed that nothing untoward was going on.

James Hewitt arrived early in his TVR sports car and immediately came through to the staff pantry. We liked him, and he knew he could relax in our company. 'Oh, James,' said Diana, blushing, as she came through. 'Sorry I wasn't at the door. I didn't hear you come in.'

The Prince was away at Sandringham, and with the boys playing by themselves outside the Princess and James went for a walk. They returned an hour later and asked for some tea. James, in cords and a casual jacket, was telling Diana a story about some party he had attended as I walked through with the tray. Both went silent as I put the things down and let them pour their own tea. The other guests had still not arrived, so I asked Chris what time he thought they should want supper. 'Let's wait and see if any other guests arrive,' he said with a knowing look.

With no nanny on, it was left to Diana to put the boys to bed herself. She bathed them and read their story before coming down to join James in her sitting room. Both were still alone. Eventually two other guests arrived and joined James and the Princess downstairs. All four had a late supper together before turning in for the night. James Hewitt was in the Blue Room with its bathroom *en suite*; the other guests were in the Green Room and the nanny's room in the nursery. The Blue Room is just a few paces away from the Princess's room.

All three guests left the following morning soon after breakfast, so I went upstairs to change the sheets. The Princess's bed looked as if it had hardly been slept in, but there were streaks of mascara on her pillow. Unusually, however, she had locked the door between her room and Prince Charles's, adjoining. William and Harry usually came in that way if they were up early, so it looked as if Diana did not want them barging through that particular day.

The Green Room was immaculate and looked as if it had hardly been used, as did the nanny's room in the nursery. It was the state of the Blue Room that surprised me. As I stripped off the sheets it became quite obvious that two people had slept in them. There were strands of hair on one of the pillows, and evidence that some sort of activity had taken place on the bottom sheet.

I looked at the sheets and raised my eyebrows. I bundled the sheets into a wicker basket and made up the bed for the next lot of guests. As far as I was concerned, it was going to be a secret.

There were to be other visits from James Hewitt over the next few months, but none that appeared to lead to such dramatic conclusions. I remember reconciling myself to the thought that if the Prince was going to lead an independent life, there was no reason why the Princess should not do so as well. After all, James was of a similar age to Diana, and the two were obviously extremely close. He was handsome and easy-going. With Charles otherwise occupied, who could have blamed Diana for seeking comfort in someone else's arms?

Charles arrived at Highgrove from Sandringham the weekend following James Hewitt's stay. Nothing was said to him about the visit, but the weekend was noticeably charged with a tension and underlying anger that could barely be disguised from the staff.

Diana waited until he had left for Italy before coming up to Highgrove with the nursery the first weekend in May. We were all invited to have Pimms in the garden with her, in an area usually out of bounds to the staff, to celebrate the start of summer. Diana was light-hearted and chatty, wanting to know what we had been up to and which television programmes we had watched. It never ceased to amaze me how such an ostensibly busy person as Diana could fit in so much television.

The Princess told fascinating stories about what she thought of stars like Michael Jackson and Elizabeth Taylor. 'You should see his nose,' she exclaimed of Michael Jackson. 'It looks as if it's about to fall off, because even with lots of make-up on you can see how thin and brittle the skin is.' She was truly impressed by Liz Taylor and said she would like to look as good as the star when she reached her age.

Diana, who sipped occasionally from a glass of Pimms throughout the evening, was not a heavy drinker, and took the drink more out of politeness than anything else. Without the Prince she was a different woman, and I remember talking to one of the policemen about how confident and assertive she was becoming. 'Yes,' he replied, pulling a face. 'Let's hope she can keep a lid on it.'

. . .

I looked at the handwritten note from Charles and had to read it several times before finally accepting that my eyes were not deceiving me. He had arranged for a new sewage system to be installed at Highgrove to cope with the increasing numbers of guests and staff. Following strict organic principles, he had agreed to a new reed-bed system that would take care of any natural raw sewage. Each of us was given a list of Dos and Don'ts, which explained how waste from the kitchen should be kept in buckets and transferred to the compost heap. Under the heading of 'Bathroom' Charles had scrawled: 'Can you please ensure that guests do not put condoms down the loo, but save them in a plastic bag.' I looked at Paul as we read it and envisaged telling some visiting king or celebrity what he should do with his condom.

The reed beds were behind the kitchen and staff car park, and were to work extremely and surprisingly well. Initially the chefs were not at all pleased, because instead of using the waste disposal grinder to get rid of food, they were now required to fill up buckets for one of the gardeners to empty on the compost heap. They had not been consulted about the change. However, despite their initial misgivings the system soon worked well, and avoided the almost yearly seizures of pipes clogged up with cream and fat that had occurred previously.

True to form, Charles was away during the early teething troubles, leaving others to break the news about changes of routine. Though no coward in other areas, he had an uncanny knack of avoiding difficult or sensitive conversations with staff or employees. It was the same higher up the social scale; in essence, if he needed dirty work done he would make sure that someone else was on hand to do it for him.

Later that month, Diana was due to travel to Hungary with the Prince. She made it very clear she was going out of duty rather than love. 'Sometimes I think I would be quite happy enough bringing up a family in the countryside,' she said wistfully one evening before she left. 'Things can really be so straightforward and simple if you want them to be.' She knew, of course, that her life could never be uncomplicated again, but still enjoyed her daydreams.

Then, on Thursday June 28, something happened that was to change all our lives at Highgrove, and show us a side of Prince Charles that we had never seen before. News came through that the Prince of Wales had fallen from his horse during a polo match at Cirencester and had broken his arm badly. He was rushed to hospital.

After we realised the condition was not life-threatening we forced ourselves to confront the next crisis: who was going to host the planned big reception at Highgrove that evening? Among those invited were Michael and Shakira Caine, just two of several dozen guests expecting to see the Prince. It was decided to go ahead – after all, the catering had been set up. Richard Aylard, Charles's private secretary, said that he would take the Prince's place.

Paul and I worked especially hard that night, moving around the assembled throng, talking to as many guests as possible and filling them in on the Prince's condition. Some had been in what they said was a state of shock when they watched the TV pictures of him coming off his horse. For a while he had lain on the ground in agony, and by-standers were worried he might have injured himself very seriously.

The following day we were told that the Prince wanted to convalesce at Highgrove, and had asked to have his office moved up there from London. Doctors anticipated that he would need about a month to recover, and we could expect to be busy. Our lives at Highgrove would never be the same.

CHAPTER THIRTEEN

Sympathy for a Broken Arm

Prince Charles lay on a specially prepared day bed in the hall, the doors on to the walled terrace at the back thrown open to allow a gentle summer breeze to waft through the house. To his right was a large white cushion, upon which he rested his broken arm. Dressed in blue slacks and a short-sleeved white shirt, Charles looked miserable and dejected. He had been let out of hospital at 11.15am on Sunday July 1, Diana's birthday, and had been driven directly back to Highgrove. Everyone tried their best to raise his spirits, but Charles seemed to be in a state of delayed shock as much as depressed.

I asked how he was as I took a glass of lemon refresher through to him in the hall. 'Bloody agony, Wendy,' he grimaced. 'But thanks for asking, all the same.'

Despite his acute pain, Charles's friends were determined that he should not be short of company. The Prince, who hates spending any great period of time alone, was subjected to a deluge of visitors, which seemed as overwhelming for him as it was for Paul and me. Every day there was one visit or another, from the P-Ts, the Van Cutsems or Geoffrey and Jorie Kent. Camilla Parker Bowles came almost daily, confirming her position as Charles's Number One friend.

That Sunday was spent quietly and morosely with Diana. 'Do you think you might have learned your lesson about polo now?' said Diana slowly, more out of pity than anger. 'Oh really, Diana,' replied Charles in exasperation. 'You don't honestly expect me to talk about that now, do you?' 'Why not?' she replied. 'It doesn't look as if you will be playing again for quite a long time.'

Despite all their problems and differences the Princess did seem genuinely concerned about her husband's injury. Although she could not resist the odd barb about a game she genuinely detested, she had noticed a flicker of melancholy in her husband's eyes that told her it might be months, if not years, before he was fully recovered.

The Prince lay on his bed and dozed, his right arm stuck out at an awkward angle. 'Such a bloody inconvenience,' he murmured as I went through to pick up his glass. 'Sorry, Sir?' I asked. 'The arm, Wendy, the arm,' he muttered.

The first few days at Highgrove after the accident passed in a whirlwind of activity. Charles found it difficult to sleep at night, and, with Diana away, slept in her double bed along with five pillows and Teddy. The bed gave him more space for the large white cushion that he carried everywhere with him for comfort, in the same way a child has a favourite blanket. Because it was so hot, and because Charles had cancelled most of his official meetings, he was able to wander around the house and gardens in shorts and casual shirts. It made quite a change from the suits and uniforms he usually wore during the week, and the baggy cords and sweaters at weekends.

Meals were set at the usual times and nearly all of them taken outside on the terrace, where Charles would sit and practise writing with his left hand. Great piles of recycled notepaper were used for this exercise, and I would hear intermittent, angry shouts of exasperation when he was having problems with certain words. 'It's like being a bloody child again,' he growled. 'God, I don't know if I am going to be able to stand this.'

Charles's arm continued to be intensely painful, and he asked for the doctor who had treated him at Cirencester Hospital to visit him at Highgrove. Gradually Dr David Mitchell, a charming man with film-star looks, became the regular duty doctor at the house. He was given a bleep and was expected to be on call twenty-four hours a day when the Prince was in residence. The main problem for any doctor was Prince Charles's reluctance to go along with modern painkillers and twentieth-century practices. Fortunately, David Mitchell took an enlightened line on such matters as homeopathic remedies, and the two men were able to communicate well.

Many of the local community brought their own herbal remedies for the Prince to try, and before long the pantry looked like a warehouse for a major pharmaceutical company. The Prince's collection of pills and lotions was beginning to rival Diana's, which practically covered her dresser's chest of drawers.

Diana had a new dresser who worked alternate weeks with Evelyn. Helena Roache, an attractive girl in her mid-twenties, had been a professional nurse and was initially flabbergasted by all Diana's potions, pills and drops. It was her job to lay out the various tablets for Diana in the bathroom, and this could occupy several hours. There were pills for the early morning, drops at 11am, a lunchtime dose, followed by yet more in the afternoon and evening.

'I thought I had a confirmed hypochondriac on my hands at first,' Helena said. 'But in fact they do seem to work. It's just a fiddle having to remember which pills are needed and when.' I thought that Diana probably needed to replace something after all the colonic irrigation she went through each month, and Helena agreed.

With the Prince out of action and very much down in the dumps, his close circle of friends had organised a rota or 'Prince sit' as they called it, and soon visitors were arriving every hour. Diane and Oliver Hoare stayed one night, followed by Nicholas Soames. Then there was Emilie Van Cutsem – later to take on an important role in the boys' lives, to Diana's annoyance. Charles adored being surrounded by his closest friends and would sit and chat with them for hours on the terrace over a glass of Pimms, or walk slowly around the gardens.

Camilla Parker Bowles, dressed casually and somewhat shabbily in a floral skirt and cotton top, would speed up the back drive and let herself on to the terrace through the Thyme Walk. Charles was always relieved to see her, taking her by the hand and kissing her firmly on the lips every time she arrived. In the early days of his convalescence they were often together with other mutual friends, forming a tightly knit set in which Diana, though invited, never felt at ease.

One day, as Charles waited on the terrace for Nicholas Soames to return from a phone call, Camilla poked her head out of the French windows and, seeing the coast was clear, whispered, 'Hello, darling. How is my favourite little Prince today?'

Charles, stripped off to the waist and wearing shorts, looked around in surprise, then, seeing who it was, laughed. The security camera was off. Thick Italian sunglasses hid his eyes. 'Take off your glasses, Charles, I want to see your eyes,' said Camilla softly.

'I am frightened to let you see what my eyes reveal,' said Charles enigmatically. 'They might give too much away.'

At that point Nicholas Soames, by now a bachelor MP again, boomed out from behind them, 'Camilla! How *good* to see you,' before moving in for a gigantic bear-hug. At over twenty stones in weight Nicholas was capable of a pretty good hug.

Camilla, with her shoulder-length hair and deep smoker's voice, seemed an unlikely mistress for Charles. Compared with Diana's beauty she could be considered exceptionally plain, and yet there was something about her that made me understand why men found her attractive. There was an earthiness about her, and a mature sense of humour, which Diana would never have. Camilla was intelligent and worldly wise, while Diana was still just a girl, however glamorous and beautiful she might look at official functions.

Charles's hatred of smoking was suspended as Camilla puffed away, putting the butts in a collection of ashtrays arranged around the terrace for her benefit. Later on Charles would let her run around after him like a wife as they invited mutual friends over for drinks and meals. Sometimes we were told not to bother to get help, but to stay in the background until everyone had left.

In the same way that Diana opened up and became more natural with her friends when Charles was away, the Prince began to put work to the back of his mind, and take comfort in the beauty of Highgrove and the pleasure of having his friends around him. Diana, who still arrived for the occasional weekend with the boys, had, as far as we knew, no idea what was going on – but I also wondered what she would have said and done had she known. I soon found out when, one morning, she walked on to the terrace and said to Charles that she was surprised Emilie Van Cutsem had stayed for a night alone.

Charles replied, 'Yes. She was here for a night a while ago,' before looking down again at his book. Nothing more was said between them, but after the Princess had moved away to the pool, Charles came into the kitchen. He stared at Paul, the butler, and me, and abruptly asked: 'How does my wife know that Emilie Van Cutsem stayed here?'

I remembered the pantry diary. Diana had been leafing through it that morning to see who had stayed. 'You mean you write everything down in there?' said Charles, a look of concern flashing across his face. 'Well, in future please do not do so. If they are private visits they should remain private and not be written down in any diaries.' With that he walked slowly back to the terrace.

Paul and I pulled a face. What were we to do? We needed to keep a record of who had been here and when for housekeeping and meals purposes. 'Thank goodness the Princess didn't ask us what else had been going on,' said Paul with a chuckle. 'I don't know what I would have told her.'

Other friends continued to congregate at Highgrove for tea and drinks with the Prince. The really close ones, including Lord and Lady Romsey and Emilie's husband Hugh Van Cutsem, stayed the night. Penny Romsey had been a girlfriend of Charles's, and since her marriage to Lord Romsey they had become two of his closest friends. Charming, witty and very attractive, Penny was the antithesis of Diana in character; where Diana was still giggly and slightly immature, Penny had an intelligent, sharper core that dazzled those who met her. Neither woman particularly liked the other, which was obvious on the rare occasions they met. Diana had an inbuilt distrust of anyone who had known Charles before her marriage, and could not cope with old girlfriends, however platonic the relationship might have become.

On Sunday July 15 the Queen paid a visit shortly after lunch. It was one of the few occasions I can remember her coming, and despite it being supposedly low-key I vividly recall the chefs flying into a panic when told about it. The Queen, who arrived dressed in a headscarf, tweed skirt and red jumper, was immediately ushered through to the terrace by Paul, who had worked for her for many years and started Palace life as the walker for her corgis.

'Your Majesty, the Prince is being so brave but is in a terrible amount of pain,' he said without being asked as they walked through the hall. 'I know he will be so pleased that you have come to visit him.' I was astounded at Paul's casual manner, and didn't detect a hint of annoyance in the Queen's tone as she thanked him for showing her through.

Prince Charles and his mother spent over an hour together on the terrace, eating daintily cut cucumber sandwiches and a specially baked Victoria sponge. Charles had put his shirt on and was sitting upright as the Queen chatted quietly with him. Both looked strangely glamorous in their sunglasses, and the conversation was punctuated with little bursts of laughter. Tigger and Roo played at their feet, and seemed to initiate a lot of conversation, the Queen at one stage picking Tigger up and looking at her closely.

The Queen Mother was a regular visitor, but the following Sunday was Prince Philip's turn, and his visits were rare. Diana, who had been at Highgrove since Thursday, decided she should go and see Fay Marshalsea, now Appleby, who had just given birth to twin sons in Somerset. Fay had been seriously ill with cancer before her marriage to Steve Appleby, and Diana had helped nurse and cajole her into good health for the wedding. Diana was learning more and more about illness and cancer through her official charity work, and knew that a visit from her would do Fay's morale no end of good.

Prince Philip leaped out of the car and dashed through into the hall. 'Charles, where are you?' he shouted as he made his way on to the terrace. The Prince looked altogether smaller and slighter than his father when the two of them stood together.

'So how are you feeling then, you old idiot?' laughed the Duke. 'Bloody stupid fall in the first place if you ask me.' I could see the Prince recoil as Philip went on to point out the reasons why he shouldn't have come off the horse. His comments were all made light-heartedly, but Charles did not appear to be feeling on top form for banter. The two men went for a walk around the gardens, and returned twenty minutes later for tea. Before very long the Duke had ordered his car and was on his way back to Windsor.

James had told me a story from his early days in the Household that illustrated the Duke's attitude towards Charles – it did not seem to have altered much. It was a few days before Christmas and the Royal Family were gathering at Windsor Castle. As usual, all stops had been pulled out for Princess Margaret, who as the pudding bowls were cleared away grandly continued her conversation with Prince Charles. She paused briefly for a sip from the glass of whisky that had been constantly refilled throughout the meal.

'It's exactly as I thought,' she barked imperiously, her fingers fiddling with a cigarette and a long holder. 'I told Lilibet at the time that something needed to be done, but would she do anything about it? Not a bit of it.' The Queen broke off her conversation with Edward and looked across at her glamorous sister, immaculate in a stunning pearl-coloured dress, replete with expensive jewellery.

'Mummy,' said Charles quietly. 'I wish you had got my ears pinned back when I was a child – it would have made life so much easier, you know. I don't think you realise quite how beastly it is to have ears like mine.' James carried on clearing away but was fascinated by the thirty-something Prince talking so candidly with his mother.

'I'm not going to go on about it, Lilibet,' Margaret continued, 'but I don't think you can deny that I told you so all along.'

'Ears? What's wrong with your bloody ears?' interrupted Prince Philip. 'For God's sake, man, pull yourself together.'

'Everyone laughed,' remembered James. Footmen jumped to attention behind each chair while the Royal Family let their napkins drop gently on to the table and floor as they made for the drawing room and one last nightcap.

.   .   .

That night Charles and Diana had supper together outside. Later she walked through into the staff pantry, where I was sitting having a drink with Harold, the butler at KP. Looking concerned, she said, 'He's still feeling pretty sorry for himself, isn't he? I do hope he gives up polo after all of this, but I fear he will keep on playing despite the accident.'

Charles and Diana had agreed to take the boys to Spain for a summer holiday, and it was decided that with his schedule more or less cleared Charles should fly over for a few days by himself before the others joined him. He was a sunlover, and was fastidious about his tan, which might come as a surprise to those who think this is solely Diana's territory. As well as packing all his clothes for the trip, Charles's valet would also have to lay out a selection of suntan oils for the Prince to choose from. Charles used to say he felt good 'within himself' when tanned, and was really rather vain about the colour of his skin. Close up, he was naturally a very handsome man, and when he was brown the whole effect was quite dazzling, showing off the blue of his eyes and the white of his teeth.

Once again, as soon as Charles left Diana returned to Highgrove with William and Harry and their new nanny, Jessie Webb. Again she threw a large barbecue in the royal part of the garden near the Chamomile Walk, for any staff who were around. She loved to see how we enjoyed being allowed into the restricted area. 'It's just like school, isn't it?' she laughed. 'Being allowed into the teachers' area as a special treat.'

That evening was the first time I met the new nanny. Jessie, a large woman like a battleship in full sail, brought a welcome air of cockney normality into the boys' lives. She was great fun, and very outspoken, which both the Prince and Princess would learn to take on the chin. She was convinced that Harry needed feeding up, and would go out on her own shopping expeditions, returning with bags full of sausages, bacon, buns and doughnuts, which she would cram into the nursery fridge. She would talk affectionately about 'that poor scrawny little thing,' making all the chefs feel guilty. 'That little boy doesn't want pasta and vegetables,' she would announce. 'He needs steak and potatoes and good stodge.'

What really upset Jessie was Charles's ability to excite the boys just as she had got them settled for the night. 'They are mental, you know,' she would say about the Prince and Princess, tapping her head. 'Those boys are going to need a lot of help if they are not going to end up as barking as their Mum and Dad.'

Diana took the boys to Spain for a week on August 12. All of us were stunned by the pictures in the papers showing a crotchety Prince of Wales alongside his photogenic, suntanned wife.

Once back from their stay with King Juan Carlos the boys travelled up to Balmoral with Charles. Diana went for a few days, but returned to London as soon as possible. She was worried about alarming developments in the Gulf after Iraq invaded Kuwait. James Hewitt, who was currently stationed in Germany, was in line to be sent there should action be taken. And for the first time in her life Diana became actively interested in politics.

Meanwhile Charles's arm was still not healing properly. He had arranged for an Australian physiotherapist called Sarah Key to come and stay at Highgrove, but first went into hospital for another operation to have a metal plate put into the upper arm. She was to move in when Charles came out of hospital on September 8. On his return he looked dreadful, and, if anything, in more pain than immediately after the accident. Despite his tan, his face looked drawn and haggard. As he limped through to the sitting room he looked as if he was carrying all the troubles of the world on his shoulders, with a large proportion of them hanging from his bad arm.

Sarah was a delightful person to have staying in the house because she was always filled with such energy. She had run a clinic off Harley Street in the past and was constantly receiving faxes and messages from patients all around the world. As far as she was concerned, Charles was going to be her main patient, and she kept him to a hard schedule. A massage table was set up in the Blue Room and she would give the Prince at least one long massage a day, before getting him on to gentle weights and an exercise bed to build up the strength in his arm. Dressed in white shorts, the Prince was subjected to a daily routine of sit-ups and chin-ups as Sarah coaxed him back into fitness.

. . .

William was nervous. He was due to start at boarding school in a few days' time, and though on the surface full of bravura and confidence, underneath he was apprehensive and concerned. Both Charles and Diana accompanied him on his first day, but unlike Diana, who moped and sulked about what they had done, Charles flew to France with Sarah Key for further rest and relaxation. From there he went straight to Birkhall, to be joined by the P-Ts and the Parker Bowleses. The day he flew to Scotland, Diana arrived at Highgrove with Harry and the nursery. She seemed low and dejected, and constantly talked about how much she was missing William. Downstairs we all told her how confident and chirpy he had looked as he shook his new headmaster's hand. 'Yes, but he is so young,' said Diana sadly. 'I can't imagine having to go through that stage of my life all over again.'

The Princess, plunged into despair because of William's departure, also had James Hewitt to worry about. There were long-distance phone calls to his barracks in Germany, and she talked anxiously at night about a land invasion of Kuwait by Allied Forces. As if to shake her troubles away, she took Harry to a local funfair in Tetbury in early October and arranged for a long heart-to-heart chat with Catherine Soames the following weekend.

After more than four weeks apart, Charles returned to Highgrove for lunch with Diana and William, who was on a break from school. Charles and Diana sat together like strangers, and focused all their energies on William, persuading him to go over every detail of his new life at Ludgrove.

'And where have you been, Papa?' he asked his father as the conversation died away. 'I've been up in Scotland walking and fishing,' replied Charles, warming to the subject. 'Excuse me, darling,' said Diana to William. 'I've just got to go and make a telephone call. I'll be back in a minute.' She left the room quickly, her face like thunder.

1991

CHAPTER FOURTEEN

Deadly Hostilities

The sound of muffled crying came from the back stairs. It was late on a Saturday night at the beginning of 1991 and I was doing my final rounds of the lights and doors before going home to the Lodge. I could stand the sobbing no longer and looked up the flight of stairs leading to the first floor. Diana, her head on her knees, was sitting on the top step, crying bitterly, her blonde hair shaking as the sobs convulsed her body.

I looked away and heard Charles shout from the sitting room, 'For God's sake, Diana, come here and talk to me.' I heard him push a chair back and start walking towards the hall. Quickly I glanced up at Diana, and could just make out her tear-streaked face in the dim light.

'I hate you, Charles,' she shrieked. 'I fucking hate you,' as she darted along the staff corridor and into her room. Diana had seen me but I didn't want the embarrassment of bumping into the Prince. I hastily moved back towards the kitchen and let myself out. As I walked down the drive I imagined Charles galloping up the main stairs and trying to get into Diana's room. I was best away from it, I thought. It was none of my business.

In emotional terms 1991 was to be the cruellest year at Highgrove so far. Over Christmas the couple had grown so full of hatred for each other that I and the other staff feared for the safety of both. However ridiculous it might sound now, I was genuinely scared that the Princess might contemplate suicide – or worse. They both found each other's company so offensive that barely a civil word passed between them.

Nobody was expected to arrive until January 18, so I went quickly around the house to check that everything was all right and that no pipes had burst. As I closed the shutters I noticed that a fax had come through for me from Richard Aylard. It was a security memo explaining that all the royal residences would shortly be on Amber Alert for at least twenty-four hours. These alerts were standard and involved a lot of common sense, such as checking all cars and deliveries. Security was always tight, but the office had regular Amber days to keep people vigilant.

There was also a long, stiff memo to all staff headed 'Economy Measures', which was deemed necessary by Charles and Diana's Private Secretary, Sir Christopher Airey. Among its numbered paragraphs was this sentence: 'It requires the kind of attitude where you turn out the lights in a room which is not being used.' The memo outlined the cost of envelopes and plastic folders, as well as reminding us how fortunate we were in having low leasing rates on household cars. I was always having to turn Charles's and Diana's lights off after they had gone, so I thought that perhaps the memo was directed at the wrong people. It also made me smile that Airey was concerned about pence when the cost of the Royal Train and royal flights ran into hundreds of thousands of pounds for the taxpayer each year.

A slightly more pleasant memo followed with a list of royal mews houses, pheasantries, cottages and lodges still available for rent throughout the year. These lodges and flats were free to some members of staff above a certain period of service, and their immediate families. Friends and girl/boyfriends were expected to pay a supplement of £3 per person per night. It was still very good value.

There was a blast of a car horn followed by the whine of a police siren. I looked out of the window and saw Harry sitting on his detective's lap at the wheel of the car, playing with the controls.

Diana jumped out as soon as the car had stopped and dashed straight past me into the sitting room. The television went on and she was just in time to catch the evening news. 'It's been like this all the way up here,' said the detective. 'She wanted the radio news on every time there was a bulletin.' Allied troops had gone into Kuwait and Diana was frantically concerned about her army friends, David Waterhouse and, principally, James Hewitt. The Princess had been corresponding regularly with Major Hewitt while he was in the Gulf, and was not above putting her staff in a compromising position sometimes by asking them to send registered post to him from their private addresses.

Diana walked back into the kitchen to join Harry and his detective at the kitchen table with me. 'Everything seems to be all right,' she said with relief. I agreed that it had been very nerve-racking. 'Nerve-racking?' snapped Diana. 'Wendy. It is more than nerve-racking when you have friends out there risking their lives.' She stayed only one night before dashing back to London after receiving a phone call from a friend. Poor Harry seemed quite bemused by all the activity.

With Diana back in London, Charles felt it safe to return. Although his arm was still a little stiff, he had practically recovered physically from the fall the previous summer, and was throwing himself into his business and social engagements.

A close bond existed between him and the former monarch of Greece, King Constantine, or 'Tino' as Charles called him. Tino would often arrive after lunch midweek, or when the Prince's diary allowed, and the two would take off for dinner somewhere. Like Prince Philip, Constantine was supposed to have a very earthy sense of humour, and outspoken Jessie would say lightheartedly, 'Where are those two off to? I don't trust them one little bit.' Whatever her intuition suggested I do not know, since there never seemed to be any sign of mischief.

I was in Prince Charles's bad books that day because I had not subliminally understood that I was meant to ask the jockey Willie Carson to stay for a cup of tea when he called in to pick up a parcel. It was a book for the Queen Mother. After handing it over to Willie, who was even tinier in the flesh than I imagined, I let him carry on with his journey. 'Wendy,' shouted Charles in a bit of a fluster as Willie drove away. 'Was that Willie Carson?' I nodded. Charles flew into a panic and shouted, 'Quick, quick, stop him. I need to speak to him.' But it was too late. As if on horseback he had sped away out of the gates. 'Really,' said Charles. 'Why didn't you ask him to stay for a while? I needed to speak to him.'

'I did, but he said he didn't have time,' I replied, probably quite indignantly.

The matter soon blew over, but was indicative of how up and down Charles's temper could be. Although he did not throw seriously unbalanced tantrums like Prince Andrew, he could still stamp his feet and go extremely red in the face if he didn't get his own way.

Terrible winds and heavy falls of snow were used as an excuse for keeping Charles and Diana apart until the end of the month. One day Richard Aylard arrived for a lunch to which fourteen Duchy guests were invited, and stayed behind with the Prince in the sitting room until late into the evening. His keenness to streamline services and staff soon won the Prince's admiration and earned him promotion within the Household.

With us Richard was scrupulously fair, but occasionally a little full of his own self-importance. He must have been in the most terrible position during the really dark months of Charles's and Diana's fighting, because he used to have publicly to deny rumours and defend the marriage. In a way it was better for us serving members of staff, because we were not allowed to talk to the newspapers, full stop, let alone have to lie through our teeth about what was really going on.

. . .

With William now away at boarding school, his parents cherished his long weekends and exeats at home. Both Charles and Diana naturally wanted to see their son, and so a compromise was reached about how long they had with him, and where they went.

Charles's reputation as an uncaring father is hopelessly wide of the mark. The day before William arrived on February 22 he was more excited about his son's imminent arrival than most fathers I have encountered. 'You know that William is here tomorrow, Wendy, don't you?' he asked me, his eyes shining brightly as he spoke of his son. 'He really is shooting up at the moment. I can't believe how quickly they grow up.'

The following day Diana and the boys drove up from London, Charles flying back in the helicopter. As it landed in the paddock both William and Harry raced down to greet him. Charles lifted both children as they jumped up to him, spinning them both around in the air despite his arm. Had such a moment been captured on film, in the way that Diana always managed, the unfair tag of Charles the bad father would never have gained credence. All three walked back towards the house, Harry jumping around his father who spoke affectionately to his elder son. Tigger and Roo yapped at their feet. It was a picture of a father and two sons totally at ease with each other.

That evening Charles and Diana had dinner with both boys in the sitting room, listening and laughing as William recounted his latest adventures. But the next day, when Charles suggested a picnic and a stroll around some old churches, Diana jumped in with another suggestion of driving to a nearby funfair, and her idea won the day. Charles looked sadly at Diana, as if she had pulled a fast one – her proposal was bound to sound more interesting to the boys than his own. I remember thinking it was slightly unfair, since what both boys would have loved would have been a day out with both their parents, not having to choose between two separate camps. However, Diana got her way.

As William grew older he was allowed to undertake more and more engagements with his parents. He was thrilled at the prospect and treated them extremely seriously. As a gesture, Harry, who was still not old enough to carry out official 'duties', was taken by Charles to visit various regiments in the helicopter. He went wild as he put on his mini-uniform and red beret, and at one stage was so excited I thought he would need to be physically restrained! Charles, who adores both boys but has a special bond with Harry, looked on approvingly as his young son proudly paraded around the house in uniform.

. . .

Now that he was fit and able again, Charles resumed his weekly 'private' excursions. On March 27 he dropped in briefly and, after bathing and changing, announced that he would be out for dinner and the night.

Diana rang, ostensibly to tell Paul how pleased she was that he would be going with her and the Prince to Czechoslovakia for their official visit. Suddenly she asked where the Prince was and Paul explained he was out. 'Where?' said Diana. 'I don't know,' answered Paul truthfully. 'Which car?' said Diana. 'The four-wheel drive,' replied Paul, and the phone went dead.

By April Diana was bringing Harry to Highgrove for riding practice whenever she had a free weekend. Charles meanwhile was travelling to and from Scotland, and reluctantly spending days in London for official engagements. Because he was basing his office increasingly at Highgrove he and his staff were forever forgetting 'essential' items in his study. If it wasn't his special pen, it was a book or sometimes even a picture. On Saturday April 6 he wanted a watercolour that he had left on his desk, and Harold, the KP butler, rang to ask if I would drive it down to London. I had had a terribly busy weekend already and at first politely refused. Eventually we reached a compromise and I agreed to meet a chauffeur at the M4 services.

'It's not really our fault,' said Harold, by way of apology. 'The Prince says he wants something and everybody has to jump. Where the wretched things are left is of no concern to him.'

After months of constant travelling, Charles settled down to official residence in Highgrove for the polo season. There were practice sessions with Major Ronald Ferguson – still resolutely maintaining his innocence about the massage-parlour scandal – and time for him to build up his confidence in the saddle after the accident of the year before. Charles was reluctantly coming to accept that he was not as young and fit as he used to be, and was suffering from aches and sprains after every practice.

Charles, who was fastidious about his looks, also had a hairdresser drive up from London every fortnight to trim his dark, thinning hair. The hairdresser was usually picked up by George, the orderly, and taken back to town – another costly round trip that never appeared to be brought to the arch cost-cutter Richard Aylard's attention.

With Charles monopolising the entertaining at Highgrove, inviting his regular set of chums as well as the headmaster of Eton, Eric Anderson, and his wife Poppy, Diana pursued her own life in London. By now she had accepted that Highgrove was Charles's territory and, since she was tired of making an effort with him and the house, saw her friends elsewhere.

Fay Appleby, who was recovering from another bout of cancer, was to have her twins christened in Taunton, Somerset, on Sunday June 2. Diana jumped at the chance to go, and arranged for several members of staff to go as well. There was an hilarious moment when she asked for a loo stop at the Crest Hotel near the M5 motorway junction. Several holidaymakers did a double-take as the Princess jumped out of the car and dashed into the loo. People looked twice and then turned to a wife or husband, who said they must be dreaming. Minutes later, as Diana returned, the same thing happened.

The service was at 10.30am and Fay was overwhelmed to see Diana and so many of her old friends. She looked dreadfully thin, but her boys were beautiful. It was a very happy occasion and Diana was in her element, fussing over the children and chatting quite naturally to all the young mothers.

I remember thinking at the time how well she handled the general public, and how charming and sweet she could be. As with any 'public' figure, a lot of it was acting and being seen to do and say the right thing, but Diana had it down to a fine art. It is such a shame that she cannot control her behaviour in private, for her real character is, understandably, nothing like the public's perception of her. I soon realised this was Diana's fundamental and potentially tragic flaw: a difficult, calculating and manipulative core of steel, expertly hidden by a marshmallow exterior.

. . .

The telephone rang in the pantry. At the same time Prince Charles received a call on his personal line. Prince William had had an accident at school and been hit over the head with a golf club. His life was not in danger, but he would need an operation. Charles ran down to the hall, his face white with shock, shouting for his coat. He looked dreadful, and paced up and down as he waited for his Aston Martin to be brought from the garage. 'I'm told it's not serious,' he explained to a group of us who stood waiting at the swing door. 'But I feel I must get down to the hospital at once to see him.' Seconds later, with the Prince at the wheel, the Aston Martin roared down the gravel drive and out on to the main road.

Although William had had an operation, he was well enough to come up to Highgrove the following weekend. He still seemed a little bit groggy and was quieter than usual. He was banned from riding in case he came off the pony and further damaged his head.

. . .

The official lunch barbecue that year was a great success and William and Harry brought friends from school. Diana, however, said she wanted a more informal one for just the Highgrove household, and this was arranged for Saturday July 6 after she had returned from Wimbledon. The Prince had gone out for a dinner party, so Diana asked for everything to be set up in the royal garden. Paul and Maria brought their two boys, Nicholas and Alexander, to play with Harry, and the rest of us sat around eating sausages and drinking wine.

Although she had written and thanked me for my birthday present

– a crystal bear – Diana came over and hugged me for remembering which animal she needed for her collection. We spoke about the boys and her engagements, and Diana revealed that she was finding it difficult to keep alert during her public appearances. 'The trouble is, I get so exhausted that all I want to do some days is sleep,' she said. I replied that I knew the feeling, and that with so many visitors all the time at Highgrove it sometimes felt like working in a five-star hotel.

Nothing was said about the Prince at all – nobody mentioned his name the entire evening. We all realised that as soon as he returned Diana would be off back to London – they had both by now perfected the art of keeping out of each other's way. The arrangement usually worked well and allowed the minimum amount of communication between them. It also protected the staff from a lot of embarrassing scenes.

CHAPTER FIFTEEN

Children in the Crossfire

Loud guffaws of laughter pealed out from the terrace. The Prince was holding a tea party for the three organisers of a forthcoming country show, and someone had just told a joke. All things considered it was a very grown-up affair, for sitting in one corner balancing a cup of tea on his knee was Captain Mark Phillips, while opposite him, his estranged wife Princess Anne was rocking her head back in laughter after a comment made by Brigadier Andrew Parker Bowles, himself one of her former escorts and the husband of Charles's mistress Camilla. The Prince, looking relaxed in cotton trousers and a short-sleeved shirt, completed the group, Diana having gone out for the afternoon.

Such a gathering seemed extraordinary considering the complicated network of relationships between them, yet at the same time wonderfully civilised. They had gathered to discuss a future event, and each one seemed totally absorbed in the subject, with no hint of uneasiness about the other members of the company. Mark Phillips, his face weatherbeaten and brown, was eating his way through a plate of sandwiches as the others discussed sponsorship and team arrangements. Anne, businesslike in light-coloured jeans and a checked shirt, watched him closely as he discussed the shape of the course.

Twenty minutes later Anne and Mark had gone, but Andrew Parker Bowles stayed behind for another cup of tea. Charles seemed relaxed and at ease with his former equerry, as the Brigadier did with him. Both possessed an enviable sang-froid as they talked about the polo that summer. The name 'Camilla' was not mentioned once.

Mandy, Princess Anne's dresser, appeared at the back door with Peter and Zara Phillips. They had come to play with William and Harry and were hoping to watch their uncle Charles play polo at the Cartier International tournament. It was a scorchingly hot day, and Diana had originally said she would take all the children to the match. However, she had heard that the place was swarming with photographers and she asked the boys if they would mind giving it a miss. 'I just don't think I can handle it all today,' she explained to them. 'We'll be followed around all over the place, and that's not much fun, is it?'

Leaving Jessie to watch over the children, who were by the pool with the Princess, Mandy and I and a couple of others took the tandem and some bikes out of the shed and headed off for a picnic. It was the most beautiful afternoon, the fields scorched yellow in the baking heat, and we soon found a perfect spot. Mandy spoke about her work at Gatcombe Park with Princess Anne, and how awful the atmosphere had been between the Princess and Mark Phillips when they were living there together. The parallels between the turbulence of Gatcombe Park and that at Highgrove were all too obvious, and the four of us worried about the state of the young royals' marriages.

Royal staff do not gossip to outsiders because it is strictly forbidden. However, when they get together it is inevitable that stories and anecdotes are exchanged. Woe betide any royal who believes he or she can keep secrets or moods from their staff, because the sad truth is they can't. One cross word to a footman in Buckingham Palace, or a putdown to a nanny at Sandringham, and the household grapevine rumbles into action.

Mandy, like everybody in royal service, had heard about Charles and Diana's rows, scenes and affairs, and like us all knew the difference between public image and private reality. 'The one tremendous thing about Princess Anne, though,' she said halfway through a peach, 'is that she, out of all of them, is remarkably consistent. If she wakes up in a bad mood then you know she is not likely to hide that from the people she meets during the day. Nothing like the "saint" you have to work for.' We laughed and nodded our heads in agreement.

The following Saturday Charles was playing polo yet again, and went on to attend a performance of *Don Giovanni* at Glyndebourne with friends. Diana, who loved opera, appeared not to have been invited, so she arranged for another barbecue to be set up, this time near the pool. As the sun began to set over the fields Diana suggested a quick game of rounders. She and Helena, her dresser, were in hysterics when it came to my turn to bat. I was absolutely hopeless, missing the ball every single time, even when Reg Spinney or Ken Wharfe, the detectives, made it easy for me. The fact that I have no ball sense at all, coupled with the infectious giggling, put me off so much that we all ended up in a heap on the ground.

It was then that Diana suggested we throw Ken and Reg into the pool, and after they were chased right round the edge of the water and chucked in, it was her turn. Diana squealed and shrieked hysterically as Ken and Reg took her by the arms and legs and threw her in, then advanced on the rest of us. Eventually everyone ended up, fully dressed, in the warm water, Tigger and Roo barking furiously at us from the side. Diana jumped out and, picking up her camera, started taking snapshots of us all, Harry, in his soaking wet T-shirt, trying to splash her as she pressed the button. She was in her element, laughing and shouting at us all as she arranged the shots, before abruptly announcing it was time for William and Harry to go to bed. That was our signal that the party was over.

I went back to the Lodge that night with very conflicting emotions. I had enjoyed myself no end and the Princess had behaved so sweetly with everybody that I felt quite overwhelmed by her. In the back of my mind, however, was a nagging doubt about her motives. I am not a cynical or calculating person by nature, but instinctively I felt there was something contrived about the whole affair, as if we were being bought off one by one by her friendliness. I discussed what I felt with a few of the others the next day, and was surprised and relieved to hear they felt the same.

Monday was to be a very busy day. Lord Snowdon was travelling up to Highgrove to do group pictures of Charles, Diana and the boys for official portraits and Christmas cards. Snowdon, a most charming and delightful man, had discussed and agreed the way he would approach the pictures with them beforehand, but at the last minute Diana decided to wear jodhpurs like the boys. Unfortunately hers were in London, and Ev was dispatched to pick them up. Hours later she returned out of breath and the Princess and the boys went upstairs to change.

A picnic hamper had been prepared along with a bowl of fruit, plates and cutlery for the outside shot under the large tree. As Snowdon finished arranging the props, which included Smokey the pony, Diana, William and Harry came out of the house in riding clothes. Charles had not bothered to dress up, and remained in his casual shirt and trousers. I am afraid the whole thing really did look exceptionally stage-managed – and the pose of happy families did nothing to convince the press. The fact that Diana was in riding gear astonished us, and we wondered if there might have been some coded message to a certain riding instructor friend who would see the pictures when they were made public.

Harry was happy to be placed anywhere and responded enthusiastically to Snowdon's and his assistant's commands. William, however, dressed in a tweed jacket and light-coloured trousers, appeared miserable, thanks to a heavy dose of hay fever. The attack came on quickly and only a few minutes into the shoot he came running into the kitchen looking for his drops. The poor boy's eyes were streaming and Snowdon, who was quite concerned, waited patiently for him to return.

Charles treated the occasion with a weary, light-hearted disdain, pointing out that he wished they could use the picture taken of him ten years ago when he was younger and had more hair. Diana, sullen and difficult earlier that day, suddenly came alive as soon as the session started, loving the pre-picture make-up, and gossiping with the hair and clothes stylists.

After the outside shots it was time to take the individual pictures of Diana that would be used for the royal Christmas cards. For these she wore a purple gown with the Spencer family tiara, later changing into a pearl-pink gown with the Queen Mary tiara. She came down the back stairs to show us her clothes, and was delighted by our reaction. She looked absolutely wonderful in the dresses, her skin glowed and she was in perfect condition. 'It's just the make-up', she said modestly. But she knew she looked terrific.

. . .

'Gosh, how wonderful, Sir! I really love your garden,' enthused the actress Emma Thompson as she chatted with Charles over an early evening drink on the terrace that day.

'Did you really plant it yourself?'

Emma was staying overnight with her husband Kenneth Branagh, and they were accompanying the Prince to the theatre in Bath. A handsome girl, she was also obviously bright, and had immediately ingratiated herself with the Prince. Kenneth Branagh was slightly more diffident than his wife, but Eric and Poppy Anderson, who were mutual friends, were there to smooth the social part of the evening. The Branaghs were staying in the Green Room, and were soon suffering from Highgrove's annual summer plague of insects.

'I simply cannot stand them,' Emma said imploringly to me. 'Surely there is something you can spray to kill them all off.' I explained that all man-made insecticides had been banned by the Prince, who took a very 'green' line on these matters.

Both seemed thrilled to have stayed at Highgrove, and actually to have had breakfast with Charles. As they left they appeared to be walking on air, like two young teenagers who had just been given an autograph by their favourite star.

. . .

The Prince and Princess holidayed together in the Mediterranean that August on board the Greek millionaire John Latsis's yacht *Alexander*. In the press the holiday, with Charles's friends Lord and Lady Romsey, was billed as a second honeymoon, but all of us at Highgrove knew that this was far from the truth. Diana had wanted to take the boys on a fun holiday, and Charles had compromised with the yacht, on the understanding that he could take his own friends with him. Diana reluctantly agreed, and was dreading the socialising on board. I later heard that she spent most of the time with the children, rarely joining in with the other adults at dinner.

When an Italian photographer finally caught up with the royal party, beating the rest of the world's press to the story, it was Diana who produced the glamorous poses, something which no doubt annoyed the rest of the group. There were front-page pictures of her looking stunning in a bikini, and performing immaculate dives into the sea.

Diana brought Harry home for many weekends, occasionally having James Hewitt over to stay as well as David Waterhouse. Harry was still at Wetherby, spending weekends with his mother and occasionally having his school friends over to play. Diana's friends, younger and less fastidious than Charles's, sometimes left tell-tale traces of their visits to Highgrove. On one occasion Charles went berserk at discovering a dog had been swimming in his favourite whale fountain on the back terrace, fouling the water. He demanded to know why the gardeners had not cleaned it out the week before. It fell to me to explain that the fountain had been cleaned, but that unfortunately a visitor's dog had got in since then. 'Which visitor?' spluttered the Prince. 'I didn't know we were expecting anyone.' I diplomatically said I wasn't quite sure who was responsible, but Charles cut me short and said: 'Don't worry, Wendy. I'll ask the Princess about it.'

The matter had obviously been discussed, and quite heatedly, before William's exeat at Highgrove in late September. Charles and Diana arrived in separate cars as usual, and communicated only in front of the children. By now William and Harry were more than conscious of their parents' problems, with poor William's face betraying a child's terrible sensitivity and awareness of how difficult things were at home. The tragedy was that both Charles and Diana deeply loved their children, while they could not stand each other's company. It was obvious that for the children's long-term happiness something needed to change radically, otherwise they would become emotionally scarred by the situation.

Unfortunately, after a period of relative strength and composure, Diana was now frequently being reduced to tears again. William bore the brunt of it, often finding his mother crying in her room. Like any young child he desperately wanted his parents to love each other, and found it difficult to take sides and apportion blame. One afternoon he found Diana crying on the back stairs and asked her what was wrong. The Princess tried to compose herself but was unable to stop her tears, saying between heart-wrenching sobs that she would explain when he was older. Suddenly Charles appeared and asked William to go into the garden with him. William, by this stage close to tears himself, turned to his father and shouted: 'I hate you, Papa. I hate you so much. Why do you make Mummy cry all the time?' He ran down the stairs and into the garden followed closely by Charles, Diana shouting at her husband: 'Now look what you have done, Charles. Why upset the children?'

Ken Wharfe was a godsend in situations like this. He knew better than most how traumatic the Prince and Princess's bickerings were to the boys, and would often magically appear at moments of crisis to take them well out of earshot. Ken was too discreet and shrewd to take sides in the domestic war, but did offer a welcome and consistent anchor for the children. 'Come on, William,' he would shout, 'let's go and have a long walk. I've got something to tell you,' taking the little boy by the arm and diverting his attention away from his parents' problems.

Charles and Diana might as well have been living in separate houses, the amount of time they spent together in the communal part of Highgrove. Charles spent the days in his garden and the evenings going over his official bags, while Diana mooched around the house, listening to music and watching TV. She seemed frustrated and restricted by her life, and would snap at staff at the slightest opportunity.

When this happened it was best to keep your head down, because she would continually try to provoke you into a full-scale argument, or simply freeze you out until she decided to speak to you again. Her dressers and nannies sometimes went weeks without being addressed by her. I once asked how they managed when she was in one of her silent phases. 'It gets bloody difficult,' replied Jessie. 'And it's also very rude. You can ask her as many things as you like to try and coax her out of it, but at best she replies in monosyllables. Usually she just ignores you.'

This was another aspect of her, in striking contrast to the sunny Diana who was such good fun at the impromptu parties and barbecues that she threw for staff when Charles was away, sending Ken out to buy quantities of Häagen-Dazs ice-cream and generally behaving like a normal, ordinary girl. Though calculating and manipulative, Diana was and is very insecure and lacking in self-confidence, which explains the sharper, bullying side of her character. Any criticism of her in the papers would lead to angry outbursts, followed by sulks that sometimes took days to blow over. Diana needed total reassurance and support in everything she did – it must have made her dressers' and detectives' lives a misery. It also made the unpredictable Diana a potential liability for the Royal Family, since nobody could read her and be prepared for what she might do.

I was getting fed up with the long hours and ghastly atmosphere in the house and wasn't sure how much longer I was going to be able to stand it. Maria, Paul's wife, knew how I felt from her conversations with her husband, but had not seen the rows and tantrums at first hand. She still found it difficult to accept that there was another side to Diana apart from the glamorous, caring individual portrayed on television and in the papers.

I was not to see Diana again until December, when all the Highgrove staff were invited to a Christmas reception at St James's Palace. She looked absolutely stunning in a dark evening gown and was excited to meet Maria's mother Betty Cosworth in the line-up as she came in, kissing her on the cheek, which upset Charles. 'Who is that woman?' he asked me later as we chatted over drinks. I told him, and he replied in a rather bemused way, 'Maria's mother? Oh, really.'

As Christmas approached, Highgrove swung into the festive season with the delivery of the fir tree. The combination of Christmas decorations, tinsel and roaring log fires created a wonderful atmosphere enjoyed more by Charles than Diana and the boys, as they tended to stay in London in the run-up to the holiday.

The weather turned nasty and Charles was unable to hunt on some days, which made him very grumpy. One morning he actually came down in his riding gear and wasn't told until the last minute that the meet had been abandoned. He stomped off back to his room in the foulest of tempers, cursing the weather and bemoaning the fact that he was unable to go riding outside. 'Why today of all days?' he shouted at Paul and me as we checked the fires around the house. 'I've been looking forward to getting out all week.'

The staff Christmas lunch was arranged for Thursday December 19 at Searcy's restaurant in London. Diana was in no mood to celebrate, since both she and Charles had come straight from a memorial service for little Leonora Knatchbull, the daughter of Lord and Lady Romsey, who had died of cancer. Diana looked depressed and downcast, but put on a brave face as we ate our way through the meal of mousseline of sole, salmon and spinach, followed by chicken Simla and then an apple, cinnamon and lemon tart.

It was a chance for everyone to let their hair down, and Charles made one of the most amusing and rousing speeches I had heard from him. There were the obvious in-jokes about various detectives and 'difficult' butlers, and he ended with his usual 'you are my ambassadors' line, which always helped raise morale. Diana, meanwhile, was complaining about a front-page article in the *Daily Mail*, which had said she would not be attending the annual Christmas party thrown by her father at Althorp that year. The *Mail* alleged that because of a long-standing feud between her and her stepmother Raine, Countess Spencer, she had decided to boycott the event to show her displeasure. Diana was confused and very angry, especially as she usually received good coverage from the *Mail*, which was one of her favourite newspapers.

'I just don't know why they have said that,' she complained. 'It is not true. William and Harry are going with me and Jessie, and it's been arranged for a very long time. Where are they getting all this rubbish from?' Of course, I had no idea, as none of us did, so all we could do was nod and shake our heads whenever it was necessary to do so. There was no use Diana's denying that she disliked her stepmother – that was abundantly obvious from the horrified expressions she pulled whenever her name came up in the papers. What really annoyed her was a story suggesting there was a tougher, more manipulative side to her character.

The following day Charles returned to Highgrove alone, leaving early the following morning for a private engagement. Maria, Lita (who worked as a cleaner in the house), and I worked all morning, getting the beds changed and washing the towels and bathmats. The Christmas tree was taken down in the hall and the house cleared of all its decorations.

'Wait a minute,' said Lita as we finished tidying up. 'Isn't it meant to be bad luck to take everything down before Christmas Day?' Maria and I laughed, telling her she could do all the work herself on Boxing Day if she liked, but as far as we were concerned we wanted to spend Christmas at home. It was only later on that I remembered what Lita had said, and how extraordinarily prophetic her warning had been. No matter how bad the problems of 1991 had seemed, they were nothing compared with the events of 1992 – the year of the separation.

1992

CHAPTER SIXTEEN

The Row about the Mercedes

The phone rang in the pantry. It was Diana, asking for a dinner tray for two. 'William and I will eat upstairs, please, and Harry will have his tea in the nursery,' she explained. 'We are all tired and William can go up to bed after he has eaten with me.'

It was the last weekend of the Christmas holiday and William was apprehensive about going back to Ludgrove. Harry had already started at Wetherby, and as a dayboy was quite happy to return. For William, however, the beginning of term was always a trauma, and an unwelcome change from his holiday routine. Although he always settled quickly once he had got over the first few days, William was and is a more sensitive and shy child than many people realise. He liked being with his mother and father, however problematical and upsetting their rows could be, and above all he loved being in Scotland and Sandringham with the court.

He and Harry had arrived with Jessie earlier that afternoon, and had raced outside in their jeans and thick sweaters to chat and play with their father, who was working in the garden. Charles knew how apprehensive his elder son became before the start of school, and spent a long time encouraging him and building up his confidence as he and Harry accompanied their father around the flowerbeds and into the potting sheds. Both boys giggled as Charles recounted stories from his own schooldays, telling them about the bullies and nasty schoolmasters of his generation.

'You've got to remember there are good and bad days for everyone at school,' he reassured William. 'You will soon settle in again once you have caught up with all your chums.' It is the sort of conversation thousands of fathers have with their young sons the night before term starts, and one over which Charles took time and care.

At 7pm Diana and her detective Ken Wharfe arrived, the Princess shouting out William's and Harry's names as soon as she was inside the house. The boys ran up to greet her, and all three then went up to the nursery for their early evening bath.

Charles walked in from outside and padded through to the kitchen where he explained that he, Diana and William would have dinner downstairs in the sitting room that evening. Paul had to tell him that Diana had ordered a bed tray for her and William in her room, something about which she had evidently not consulted Charles.

'Are you sure?' said Charles quietly. 'I thought we were all going to have dinner together this evening.' He picked up the phone and rang through to the nursery. His face looked troubled and perplexed as he spoke to his wife. 'Right,' he said softly. 'Well, will you please tell them that I will be up to say goodnight in a moment.' Charles ate his supper alone, William and his mother eating theirs in bed together with the television on.

Diana's decision to have the meal in her room was a cruel blow for the Prince, and an increasingly common stunt she would pull to keep William and Harry away from their father. We used to think it disgraceful how she would involve the boys in the marital politics, no matter how unhappy she was with Charles. She knew Charles would be left alone downstairs. It did little for the atmosphere in the house and ultimately was not doing her sons any good, as they became caught between both parents. Such behaviour also seemed so unfair, considering her own childhood. Diana, herself the victim of a broken home, must have known the dangerous emotional effects on young children, but didn't appear to have learned from her own experiences.

That evening Jessie seemed very fed up as we chatted in the dining room over a glass of wine. Sandringham had been 'an absolute disaster'. 'The Princess spent most of the time crying,' she said, shaking her head slowly. 'And of course the boys were spoiled rotten by the court. I just don't know why she keeps on going up there with the Boss if it is so miserable for her.'

Of course, we all knew the problems. Diana hated holidaying with the Queen and the main Buckingham Palace household because she felt uncomfortable in such a large group of people. Jessie said that Diana had hardly spoken to anyone and locked herself away in her room to listen to music and watch television.

'It's almost as if there is no turning back for her now,' said Jessie. 'How can she ever be expected to be one of the main group again, having behaved so strangely in front of them all for so long?' All of us listened quietly as we were told how Diana, close to tears, had hurriedly left one meal with the other royals, leaving Charles bewildered and embarrassed by his wife's behaviour. We were beginning to understand that she felt an outsider in their company, and could not help but react in an emotionally volatile way any time she felt under pressure.

Unlike Fergie, who was perfectly at ease in big social gatherings, Diana found the prospect of large house parties intimidating. It was easier to drop out of everything rather than suffer the humiliation of not feeling totally accepted by the people around her. Added Jessie, 'With the boys joining in with the other children she literally has nothing to do or interest her. The whole time there was grim for everyone concerned.'

The following morning Diana took William out shopping with Ken Wharfe, returning to Highgrove with a large fish platter she had bought for her mother. William had bought a Mr Bean video, and since their father was out for the day both boys watched it with their mother in the sitting room during the afternoon. Charles would have been horrified to hear that his sons had spent the day in front of the television. He frequently asked them to switch it off if he caught them watching during the day. When this happened, Diana allowed William and Harry to use the set in her bedroom, both boys darting up the back stairs by the staff dining room to avoid being detected by their father.

Harry was usually in bed by 9pm and William allowed to stay up a little later. Since this was to be William's last night at home before school, he came down for supper with his father in the sitting room, Diana having her own bed tray upstairs again in her room. Quite what William thought of this arrangement I do not know, but it certainly seemed painfully sad that the parents could not bring themselves to eat together for their son's last night at home.

The one thing that did bring them together, however, was William's reluctance to go back to school. Diana was taking him back that Sunday soon after lunch. William came into the kitchen to say goodbye to me and Paul, trying desperately to fight back the tears. It was heartbreaking to see him, and both Paul and I embraced him and said we were all looking forward to seeing him again soon for his first exeat.

Everyone tried to cheer him up, but it was no use. By now the tears had started to roll down his face and several of us felt close to tears ourselves, which was the last thing he needed. Charles called out to him from the hall, and gave him a long hug as Diana waited to get into the car. Both talked quietly and affectionately to their son as he said how much he wanted to stay at home.

'I know exactly how he feels,' said Charles to me as the car pulled away. 'I went through exactly the same feelings myself before the start of every term. It doesn't make it any easier, of course, being who he is. Life can be made so very difficult.'

Charles went out for dinner alone that night and returned well after midnight, despite having a 7am call the following morning. Diana rang soon after he left and asked to speak with the Prince. She seemed surprised that he had gone so early, and didn't appear to have any idea at all about his movements. 'I don't know what is going on,' said Paul when I told him about the call. 'That poor girl.'

I had asked how William was when Diana rang and she said she was very concerned about him. 'It's so difficult for him, Wendy,' she said. 'I don't think anyone really understands what it's like being caught up with the Royal Family.' I thought her choice of words strange. 'Caught up' seemed to imply that their position in society was almost a curse, rather than a privilege.

'Anyway, there are going to be some changes soon,' said Diana. 'And one of the first is going to be my new car. You'll see when I come up the weekend after next.'

Charles spent alternate nights at Highgrove while Diana stayed in London. With William away at school she had no need to come up to Gloucestershire, and was certainly not going to spend any days alone with her husband – their relationship had moved on from that stage. Charles therefore entertained his own friends, and hosted drinks and dinner parties for people involved in Duchy business. This meant we were all very busy at Highgrove, renting tables and chairs locally for the larger events, and preparing the guest rooms for overnight stays by personal friends. As in previous years the arrangement worked well. There was no tension and both the Prince and Princess were able to pursue their own lives apart.

We were growing used to this routine now, and knew what to expect when Diana, William and Harry arrived on Saturday February 1 in her brand-new cerise red Mercedes sports car. Diana was ecstatic about the new car and showed it off proudly to everyone in the back yard. William, glad to be away from school for exeat, and Harry were jumping in and out of it, pleading for Ken to raise and lower the roof so many times that he thought it might break.

Diana told us that, despite all the criticism in the press of her buying a German car, she was determined to keep it. 'I really don't see what all the fuss is about,' she told us as we looked at the leather upholstery and listened to the sound system. 'It's wonderful, isn't it?' She added, 'I don't care what they say, I am going to keep it. Why can't I have the car that I want?'

She asked if anyone wanted to go for a ride in it, and took several of us out for a quick spin. Diana had obviously been taught certain driving skills by her personal protection officers, since we took off at breakneck speed. Dressed in jeans, a jumper and a baseball cap, she really knew how to put the car through its paces, taking corners at over 60 mph and loving the nervous laughter and gasps of fear from the back seat.

In her euphoria at getting the car of her dreams, Diana had not counted on Charles's reaction. He thought the Mercedes obscenely insensitive at a time of widespread recession and unemployment, pointing out that at least his Aston Martin was British. That evening he and Diana almost came to blows over the wretched thing, causing Diana to stomp off for a long walk by herself in the fading light. With her hands thrust deep into her puffa jacket pockets and her Walkman clamped tightly around her ears, she set off alone to the furthest corner of the estate. When her detective, Peter Brown, asked where she was going, she replied, 'For a bloody walk, Peter, so please don't follow me.'

The police were always in a quandary when this happened, because officially someone should have been with her at all times. However, on this occasion, as on others, it was more pragmatic to let her get on with it, and just hope she came back within an hour. If that didn't happen the officers went out to look for her discreetly, pretending they were simply going out for a walk themselves if they came across her returning.

Although Diana's mood was now much better since her row with Charles, she was not prepared to sit down for dinner with him. Once again she requested a bed tray, asking Jessie to get Harry bathed and ready for bed. She told Jessie that she would take care of William, since he would be having supper again with her.

The following morning Diana asked for breakfast to be taken upstairs to the nursery, where she and the boys would be eating. Charles, upset by the fact that William had had supper with Diana in her room, could barely contain his anger when he discovered his wife's breakfast arrangements. He rushed upstairs to the nursery and asked to speak to Diana in the sitting room. The Princess refused to come down, leaving Charles to breakfast alone with his copy of the *Sunday Times*.

Later that morning, as Diana and William watched Harry go for a short ride on his pony, I helped Jessie clean the nursery bathroom and make the beds. 'She hasn't spoken to me since Christmas, you know,' she grumbled as we changed the sheets on Harry's bed. 'I have absolutely no idea what's wrong with the daft girl. She just picks people up and then drops them for no apparent reason at all.'

I asked Paul what was behind the latest tiff and he said darkly that Diana thought Jessie had 'betrayed her trust', whatever that meant. I explained to him that Jessie didn't know what she had done to upset Diana, to which Paul replied, 'Who does, half the time?' The whole situation seemed so silly and unsatisfactory, with Diana gossiping and telling her butler one thing, yet not being strong enough to confront Jessie with her grievance. I decided to keep well out of it.

That afternoon, after the most gruesome lunch together where hardly a word was passed, Diana returned to London with the boys. She was in floods of tears as Peter Brown took the wheel, William and Harry sitting subdued and confused in the back seat. The Princess tried to wipe her eyes dry with a tissue as William put a comforting hand on his mother's shoulder. It was very foggy outside and as Peter turned on the car's lights I saw Diana put her face in her hands. Prince Charles did not come out to say goodbye. He was on the phone to his office at St James's, leaving at 4.30pm for a dinner with the prime minister, John Major.

Charles had promised to take Paddy Whiteland out to celebrate his seventy-ninth birthday, and on Thursday February 6 he took the old rogue out for a hunt supper and get-together at Badminton. Paddy, who is Charles's eyes and ears at Highgrove, had been looking forward to the occasion for weeks. Although he was growing weaker with age, he had lost none of his humour and Irish devilment. He would chase me around the house and pinch me whenever he could, and made his thoughts quite plain to the Prince on the subject of Diana. It wasn't so much what he said about her, it was the way he paused and then shook his head with a sigh every time her name came up.

'They're 'aving to go off on some foreign jobbie,' said Paddy shortly before the Prince arrived to take him out. 'I shouldn't think that's going to go down too well with his Nibs.' Paddy had listened to Charles's innermost thoughts on Diana, and was not one to mince words, regardless of who was hearing them. He had also seen a whole string of girlfriends pass through Highgrove before the Prince married, and was often telling us what a bad choice he had made in Diana. 'Too much of a silly little girl for the Prince,' Paddy would say dismissively. 'What the Boss needs is a woman.' And Paddy, as we all knew, was aware of who the Prince's special women were.

As Paddy had predicted, Charles was in a bit of a state the morning he left for Oman. He was due to link up with Diana later in India, and on his last morning at Highgrove before the flight was more than a little tetchy. He was shouting at Ken Stronach, his valet, from quite early in the morning, asking where his bone shoehorn was. Ken looked carefully for it and found it under the armchair where it usually lived. Anyone could see it, of course, apart from the Prince, who was having one of his obstreperous turns.

He then started complaining about his mattress, which he said was not hard enough, but which had been too hard the week before. Ken raced around upstairs like a man possessed but still didn't have enough arms or hands to keep up with the Prince's demands. Finally it was my turn. Charles appeared at the kitchen door, a rare sighting of him in staff quarters, with Tigger in his arms. 'Wendy,' he said abruptly. 'I think Tigger is ill. Make sure she gets the best treatment available. Ring the vet and make sure he gives her a proper check-up.' I realised that Charles was working himself up into a state, fussing like a mother over her young children the first time she left them alone. I told him I would call the vet as soon as he had gone. 'Thank you so much, Wendy,' he said, his face breaking from an anguished sweat into a weak smile. 'I would hate anything to happen to her.'

As the Prince drove away with his private detective, staff and back-up, we all breathed a huge sigh of relief. 'What did I tell you,' laughed Paddy. 'He'd rather do anything in the world than spend some time with her – and who could blame him?'

A week or so after Diana returned from India, Jessie brought Harry and William to Highgrove. It was William's exeat weekend and Diana was anxious for both boys to be together. Once again Diana asked for a bed tray for herself and William, getting the nanny to put Harry to bed earlier in the nursery.

William was shooting up in height and seemed more grown-up and mature than I had seen him before. But he also seemed more subdued and sad. I was concerned about him, as were several other staff. 'Of course, it can't help, having two parents who are both off their rockers,' quipped Jessie. Although it was meant as a joke, several of us thought there was more than a grain of truth in what she said.

Charles was out visiting friends and did not return until well after 10pm. As he came in he asked if the Princess was in, and was told she had gone to bed. 'Ah,' said Charles ironically. 'How convenient.'

Before Charles left for another skiing holiday he stopped off at Windsor for the weekend, and word soon reached us along the Palace grapevine that he had spoken to the Queen about his marriage. The conversation had apparently been calm and dignified, but the subject of an official separation had been mooted. Such an idea seemed horrific to all of us at Highgrove. However bad their domestic life, we never thought the Prince would consider separation an option. I was told the Queen had asked him to persevere and not to raise the issue again for at least another six months. It was very gloomy news, we thought at the time, but perhaps the only solution.

Charles was still away when Diana and Harry arrived for the week-end on March 6. The first I heard of them was Diana storming through the back door cursing loudly. She had been spotted by a photographer on a bridge on the M4 in her new Mercedes and was preparing herself for a public storm of protest about the car. 'Fucking press!' she repeated, several times. 'Why can't the bastards just leave me alone?' Dave Sharp, one of her detectives, was trying to calm her down as she ranted in the kitchen, telling her that perhaps the picture would not be used. 'Of course they'll use it,' shouted Diana. 'Don't be a bloody idiot.'

As she slowly calmed down I saw Evelyn dart quietly upstairs. She looked more depressed than I had seen her for months, so I quickly excused myself and went up to her room. Ev was sitting on her small bed on the verge of tears. I asked her what was wrong.

'I don't think I can carry on much longer,' she said wretchedly. 'My life is being made a misery, and I just don't know what to do.' I took her in my arms and let her pour her heart out to me. In fits and starts she sobbed, 'She just won't speak to me any more. And when she does she is so rude that I think she wants me out for good. I have given her so much of my life. I worked for her right at the beginning and have sacrificed so much. For what... just to be thrown out as a piece of rubbish when she feels like it. Nobody knows what she is really like. She can be so cruel.'

The weekend was to deteriorate. The morning papers that Saturday had front-page pictures of Diana, Dave Sharp and Prince Harry in the car, accompanied by critical pieces about her driving a Mercedes. 'Bastards,' screamed Diana when she saw the pictures, ripping out the offending pages and throwing them on the fire. 'What on earth has it got to do with them!'

Dave Sharp tried to reason with her, but eventually gave up. Later he explained another worry, that Diana had not even thought about. 'We were going at about 85 mph when they caught us,' he said. 'The picture is so clear and good, even at that speed. What would have happened if it was a gun instead of a camera pointing at us from the bridge?'

The sound of high-pitched shouting came from Diana's room. I had just finished checking the nursery, and could hear Diana shrieking at Evelyn about something she had left behind at Kensington Palace. 'The styling brush, yes, the styling brush, idiot,' she yelled. 'But you haven't used it for six months,' replied Ev meekly. 'Get out,' stormed Diana, slamming the door.

I helped a very tearful Ev back to her room, but as we got inside her phone went.

'Yes, it's me, Evelyn,' the receiver squawked. 'Go into town and get me one. I don't care where you have to go so long as you come back with what I want.' The phone was slammed down. I walked Ev quietly down the back stairs and out to the car. She was gone for well over two hours, and when she returned with a brush, Diana had decided against using one after all.

CHAPTER SEVENTEEN

Public Revelations

Unprecedented tantrums by the Prince of Wales that month suggested that, like Diana, he too was beginning to crack under the pressure of a highly unsatisfactory marriage.

Both Charles and Diana were off to Europe for a couple of days, Charles to Berlin, Diana to Budapest. The Prince was leaving from Highgrove and the Princess from London, and an early morning phone call from Diana to her husband had put him in the foulest of moods. He had taken the call shortly after 8.30am in the dining room and slammed the phone down in disgust a few minutes later. Then, pacing up and down in his bedroom, he had attempted unsuccessfully to dress himself in the stiff uniform of one of his regiments. Ken Stronach, who would usually have helped Charles with the trickier studs and buttons, had flown on to Berlin in advance, leaving Charles cursing and stamping his feet like a spoilt schoolboy.

When he did eventually descend the stairs, Paul said how smart he looked in his uniform, which led to another explosion. 'No I don't. It's horrible. I hate it. It's so uncomfortable,' screamed Charles before rushing up to his bedroom again. Seconds later the phone went in the pantry. 'I want Ken,' he shouted. 'I don't believe it... Where are my special bloody cufflinks? Ken should know by now NOT to pack every-thing and leave me stranded by myself.' Paul, who was holding the receiver away from his ear at arm's length, timidly offered to come up and help. 'No,' screamed Charles. 'No, No, No. I want Ken.' The phone went dead.

I had rarely seen him in such a temper, and we crept around the house doing our duties as quietly as possible. Charles was not due to leave until 10.15am, and fortunately by the time I had walked upstairs to check the linen cupboard he had calmed down sufficiently to have a more civil conversation. He passed me on the deep-pile green carpet looking hot, bothered and ferocious. Suddenly he stopped and actually apologised. 'I'm so sorry about this morning,' he said rather meekly. 'It's been a bit of a difficult morning.' Then, as he started to walk down to his waiting car, he added, 'Thanks a million, Wendy. I know how hard you all work for me.'

It quite transformed the day. Unlike Diana, who could be sullen and moody for weeks, Charles's tantrums were a storm in a teacup. Up in the air screaming with rage one minute, he could normally be relied on to be back at ground level within the hour. The fact that he had apologised, and seemed truly embarrassed about his behaviour, showed a more balanced character than his wife. I wished him a good trip, and Charles thanked me with a smile and a wave as he left.

Friends of mine who stayed at the Lodge would often be intrigued to come across the Prince on his knees in the mud. One Saturday in early April I had a houseful, and we all decided to go for a walk. As we skirted the house, one of my guests pointed to a dishevelled-looking man, head bowed in the drizzle, pulling out weeds from a herbaceous border. 'Does the Prince have gardeners here all the time?' she asked. 'Can't they go inside when it rains?' I looked across and saw who the 'gardener' was. She was quite shocked when I told her it was Prince Charles. 'Gosh, I hope he didn't hear me,' she giggled. 'Fancy me thinking the Prince of Wales was a gardener.'

Charles was retreating more and more into his garden when he stayed at Highgrove, as if it was the only source of comfort he could find. On some days he looked quite desperately sad as he paced around, digging and weeding, barely saying a word to anyone. 'Look at him,' said Paul. 'All he thinks about is the wretched garden.' He sounded just like the Princess.

Charles and Diana were not together again at Highgrove until

William's exeat from Ludgrove on Friday May 8. And then the couple barely exchanged a word, Charles busy with his polo and Diana taking the boys back to London before he had a chance to speak to them. It had been quite a heartbreaking Saturday. The Prince had not arranged to play a chukka until that afternoon at Cowdray Park, and arrived at breakfast that morning expecting to see William and Harry. After half an hour he rang through to the pantry and asked where the boys were, to be told by Paul that they were both having breakfast with their mother in the nursery. As Charles got up from the dining room he bumped into Diana and the boys heading for the back door, both children clutching water pistols and dressed in their army gear. 'Where are you going?' said Charles.

'We are going back to London. What does it look like?' snapped Diana, as she bundled the boys into the car. The Princess had obviously hoped to smuggle the boys away without her husband realising, and so as not to upset them Charles appeared to take the decision to avoid a traumatic scene. 'This is ridiculous, Diana,' he said quietly, his voice laced with anger. 'What on earth are you playing at?'

'We are going to London. Why don't you get ready for your precious polo,' she replied curtly. Later that morning Charles left with his detective, spending the night away from Highgrove at a private address.

With both Charles and Diana away I began to take stock of how badly I was being affected by all the problems at Highgrove, and the hours required of me. I had already passed my sixtieth birthday, and the last thing I needed as I crept around Highgrove at 7am was a couple in the throes of a bitter marriage wrangle. Sad though such break-ups are for the parents and children concerned, the disintegration of a royal marriage spreads an altogether wider net. The people who are on call for the royals at all times are affected just as badly as blood relations, sometimes more, considering the loyalty the Prince and his family inspire in people.

I seriously wondered about throwing in the towel. I was not confident that I would manage on my savings, however, and as the office at St James's Palace had asked me to stay on for at least another couple of years, I resigned myself to the situation. Who knows, I thought to myself. It could just be another bad patch they are going through. Another baby perhaps, and everything will be back on an even keel. But of course, it wasn't to be.

The Prince and Princess had attended Expo 92 in Spain on May 21, looking more miserable together than ever before in public. The pictures of them both looking bored and resentful flashed across the world, proving to everyone what we had kept a secret for so many years. 'They can't even bother to put on a show now,' said Paul, shaking his head slowly as we looked at the morning papers. The pictures showed them sitting on adjoining chairs at a public ceremony, but they were thousands of miles apart. The gulf that separated them in private was finally showing in public. Whatever their press spokesmen suggested, nothing would change the public's interpretation of those shots. The game was up. There was no use in their pretending any more.

For the sake of the children Charles and Diana took the boys to the Isles of Scilly for a few days after the Spanish fiasco, Charles returning to Highgrove a day before the Princess flew into London. The following day he invited Lord Romsey over for supper. He was one of the Prince's closest friends, and usually the two men were light-hearted and relaxed together. That Bank Holiday evening on May 25, however, Romsey and the Prince appeared subdued and sombre. There had been rumblings in the press about a forthcoming biography of Diana that promised to 'paint the true picture' of her troubled marriage to Prince Charles. The two men had a drink together on the terrace before having supper inside in the sitting room. They stayed up late, discussing something so secret that they spoke *sotto voce* behind closed doors.

That night Lord Romsey stayed in the Green Room, joining the Prince for breakfast. Neither looked as if they had slept very well. 'Let's just wait and see what happens, Charles,' said Lord Romsey as he left that morning, thanking Paul and me for looking after him. 'Things might not be as bad as feared.'

But of course, they were – far worse than anyone could have feared.

.   .   .

Charles was being fed information through his press office about likely revelations in the new royal biography, and it sent him into what can best be described as a panic. Eric and Poppy Anderson were asked over for dinner on May 29. They spent hours locked away with the Prince in the sitting room, despite its being a gloriously hot day outside. No one knew quite what was going on, apart from the fact that the *Sunday Times* was due to publish a first instalment of the Andrew Morton book on June 7.

Lord Romsey returned to Highgrove for another overnight stay on June 5 and Charles had his friends, the interior designer Robert Kime and his wife Helen, staying on Saturday night, which caused an awkward Sunday morning when the paper first appeared. Charles had arranged for his press secretary, Dickie Arbiter, to fax him the relevant pages as soon as they came out, and since the paper was deliberately held back they were not sent until 5.26am on the Sunday morning. Dickie, a pleasant and jolly former radio reporter, apologised for the delay with the fax, and had obviously been up half the night waiting for the paper to arrive.

That morning at breakfast the photocopied and faxed pages were placed at the head of the dining room table for the Prince to look at. The atmosphere was not made any easier by there being guests around, and the conversation seemed a little stilted, to say the least.

Diana was not down for more than a few minutes before she made an excuse and withdrew to her room. Charles, however, stayed seated at the head of the table and read through all the material, before getting up and going for a stroll around the garden with the Kimes before they left.

I was amazed by the Prince's self-control, since the article was worse, far worse, than anybody had thought it would be. Several of us had of course seen the pages lying on the fax machine earlier that morning, and had had a chance to look through what had been written. In the staff areas everyone spoke in a hushed whisper, not sure what to say or do. Several members of staff loyally declared they would never read the book or buy the *Sunday Times* again. But, of course, as the day continued others made excuses to go out and buy copies of the paper secretly.

After seeing his guests off, Charles walked upstairs to the Princess's room, carrying the faxes with him. Within minutes Diana was running downstairs and out to her car, her face covered with a deep blush, her eyes brimming with tears. She was going back to London, she said, and dashed out of the door.

Charles, meanwhile, walked slowly around the garden by himself for over an hour before going upstairs to dress for polo. He did not return until much later that evening, and had obviously had more than his abstemious one glass of Pimms after the match. 'For goodness' sake don't mention anything about the story,' said Paul sternly to us all. How stupid, I thought. As if anyone would!

It was several weeks before I saw Diana again. The newspapers had been full of in-depth analytical pieces about who was behind the Andrew Morton book, and more importantly why.

When the Princess did arrive that Friday she came with her detective Dave Sharp, Evelyn Dagley, Harry and his detective Reg Spinney, and Chris Barber, the chef. Diana looked tense, but pleased to be out of the public spotlight, and said she wanted a quiet weekend with Harry. The Prince, she said, was not expected. According to our schedule he was due that Saturday, but nonetheless Diana was adamant that her information was correct. Because of this she arranged another staff barbecue, and asked Dave Sharp to organise it in the royal part of the garden. As Dave was preparing the charcoal Ken Stronach suddenly pulled up in a household car, and announced that the Prince was due in thirty minutes.

Diana looked at us darkly, and went into the house as everything was transferred to the stable yard at the back of the house. Charles, however, had not come to stay, but only for a bath and a change of clothing. As Diana joined the rest of us the Prince, fresh and smelling of cologne, walked past the group and into the garden to pick a bunch of sweet peas. Ken told us he was going out for a birthday party that evening and was not expected back at Highgrove until the following day. All eyes were on him as he walked up to Diana and took her quietly to one side.

'I didn't think you were coming this weekend,' he said with barely disguised hatred in his voice. 'You told me, Diana, that you would not be here.' With that he walked purposefully back along the gravel path and into the house. Diana was more subdued than before when he had left, and seemed unable to recover her equilibrium. She kept her eyes downcast throughout the rest of the evening, rushing inside to make a series of phone calls, then returning with red, puffy eyes.

By turning up that evening Charles had wrecked Diana's hopes of a peaceful weekend, and spoiled his own mood as well. Each seemed as upset as the other that their visits had coincided.

Diana was up early the next day and left with Harry to collect William from school. It was his tenth birthday and a party had been arranged for him in the King of Greece's garden in Hampstead Garden Suburb. Charles planned to join them independently and then go and play polo, before spending the night alone at Highgrove.

There must have been a special arrangement with Ludgrove

School, because the Princess took Harry over to see William again the following Sunday for a picnic. She and her son had stayed at Highgrove the night before, but Charles had not been around, which allowed her to relax in the pool and speak to friends on her mobile phone. Diana seemed brighter than the weekend before, and was positively friendly as we chatted that Saturday afternoon in the kitchen. 'William is a bit homesick,' she confided. 'I do worry about him so much.'

The old adage that when it rains, it pours was never truer than the weekend of Friday July 3. The foal of the Prince's favourite horse, Reflection, slipped in a hole in the paddock, breaking her leg, and had to be put down. Paddy was in a terrible state, blaming the stockmen for putting in cattle, which then churned up the ground. The Prince was beside himself with grief – the foal had been the first to be born at Highgrove. He demanded to hear all the details but did not blame Paddy, sending him a note the following day telling him not to hold himself responsible for the tragedy.

Thus the arrival of Diana and the boys on the Saturday did little to raise Charles's spirits, and the atmosphere of pent-up tension was compounded by the arrival that evening of his friends Hugh and Emilie Van Cutsem, who were going to the theatre with him. Diana took William up to bed with her that night at eight o'clock, both of them ordering a dinner tray and intending to spend the evening watching television.

That Sunday there was another newspaper story to cause concern to Charles, this time by one of Diana's masseurs, Stephen Twigg. Unlike the previous occasion when the Princess had remained publicly silent about the *Sunday Times* serialisation, she let out a gasp of horror at the new revelations.

'I do think it's getting a bit too much, Diana,' said Charles drily, in what must be the understatement of the century. 'Are there any of your friends who are not talking to the newspapers?'

Diana had been due to see Stephen Twigg for treatment that evening at Kensington Palace after attending the Wimbledon men's final. Evelyn was told to ring him up and cancel the appointment. As she left, Diana told me how inconvenient it was for her when people broke her trust. 'It means I am going to have to find someone else now,' she said quietly. The fact that she was filling thousands of newspaper column-inches worldwide, thanks to a group of her friends talking to a writer, did not seem either to occur to or bother her.

The Prince and Princess's public rift was now of great concern to the Palace old guard. Diana's grandmother, and a close friend of the Queen Mother, Ruth, Lady Fermoy, stayed overnight with Charles to discuss the situation. Lady Fermoy, by now frail and drawn, had been horrified by Diana's involvement in the book, and walked slowly round the garden with the Prince. She, like everyone else, knew that the problems were now insoluble, and wanted to help Charles through the crisis. Her visit appeared to comfort and help prepare the Prince for the ultimate collapse of his marriage.

He also took advice from his close friends Amanda and Gerald Ward, whose daughter Sarah worked in the St James's Palace office. Gerald was one of Charles's equerries, close enough to the Prince to be able to talk candidly about private matters. Another source of comfort was the Prince's mentor Sir Laurens Van Der Post, who paid several daytime visits to Charles at Highgrove. The two men walked for hours, deep in conversation, and also attended the theatre together. I remember being fascinated by Sir Laurens's craggy face and whispy white hair. I knew that the Prince relied heavily on him. But as I looked at this deeply intelligent, wiry old man I could not help worrying about how the Prince would react when he was no longer around.

Charles was at his lowest ebb, devastated by the publicity about his relationship with Diana, and needed constant support. Worse was to come with the publication of a taped conversation between Diana and her friend James Gilbey, and at one stage we seriously wondered whether the Prince would be able to carry on. The hotline between Highgrove and the Queen rang more often these days, and conversations frequently ended in sharp, acrimonious exchanges.

Nonetheless, Charles's spirits had lifted a little by September, when Sarah Key made another visit to Highgrove for deep physiotherapy on his knee. She accompanied him to Balmoral and travelled with him around the country, bolstering his confidence and providing him with a perfect antidote to the shock of Diana's terrible breach of trust. 'Let's get you completely fit again, Sir,' she would joke. 'You're going to need to be in tip-top condition to pull through this one.'

CHAPTER EIGHTEEN

Final Separation

Diana was in floods of tears in her room. She had somehow heard about a tray of jewellery specially prepared for the Prince to look over regarding his choice of Christmas presents that year, and had been mortified by the allocation of gifts. Whereas a diamond necklace had been marked down for Camilla Parker Bowles, she had discovered to her horror that she was due to receive a collection of cheap paste jewels.

'I don't want his bloody fake jewels,' she cried. 'I thought cheating husbands took great care to keep their wives sweet with the real things, saving the tawdry stuff for their tarts.' She was inconsolable, and vowed bitterly that she would never be able to forgive Charles, for anything.

The Princess had run the gauntlet of bad publicity for several months, with the publication of an alleged tape recording of a conversation between her and a debonair second-hand car salesman called James Gilbey. His name was not familiar to us at Highgrove, since he had never visited Diana, as far as we knew, at the house.

That autumn the Princess pulled out of planned arrangements at the last minute, pleading exhaustion, and was generally ill at ease and vulnerable. We were surprised when on November 18 she announced that instead of joining the Prince and his family at Sandringham, she would stay at Highgrove with William and Harry. This last-minute change of plan threw the normally efficient staff rota into chaos, since instead of one chef on duty, two were now needed: one for Charles and another for her. Paul, however, did not seem surprised and finally admitted that he had known of her decision for weeks. 'She told me she just couldn't face being with him,' he explained. 'Things have got so bad now that she's not able to be in the same house, let alone the same room as the Prince.'

Harry had started at Ludgrove School with William and both boys had an exeat that weekend. On Thursday November 19, therefore, Diana and the boys drove straight to Highgrove, leaving the Prince and his friends to enjoy a shooting weekend in Norfolk. Royal entertaining at Sandringham was more lavish than in any other household, and Chris Barber, the chef, seemed quite pleased to be away from it all in Gloucestershire. Diana, too, appeared calm and reserved, happy to have her boys to herself.

That Friday Diana sat in the kitchen with William and Harry and chatted to Paul and me about her recent trip to Korea with the Prince. Media coverage had shown a couple at war, and I was surprised that she brought the subject up in front of us and the boys. 'I was so tired, I could hardly cope,' she admitted. 'The whole trip was really a mistake. No wonder I looked so miserable in the pictures.'

That evening the Princess put the boys to bed and returned to the sitting room, where she and Paul spent nearly half an hour deep in conversation. 'Something's brewing,' said Paul quietly as he came through to the pantry. 'I can't quite put my finger on it but I just feel we are on the verge of some terrible news.'

The next day Diana had arranged for a special treat for William and Harry, and all her time was given over to her sons. A lorry turned up at the back courtyard in the pouring rain and deposited two motorised go-karts for the children to drive around the estate. Despite the weather the young princes jumped at the chance and were soon racing each other around the lanes, going at what seemed breakneck speeds in the appalling conditions. The Princess shouted encouragement from the back yard, her waxed jacket dripping with rain, her face flushed with excitement and the cold.

Neither she nor the boys were bothered in the slightest by the weather, and all seemed reluctant to cut short the fun for lunch. 'We'll have lunch all together in the staff dining room,' said Diana excitedly as she helped me lay the table. 'Then we'll continue with the karts.'

That lunchtime the Princess took great delight in serving us drinks and offering more food. She was like any other normal young mother, chatting informally with everyone there and appearing so natural that it must have come as a shock to the couple who had driven over with the go-karts. Chris did all the food, and joined in with the fun. 'I'm so glad I'm here rather than at Sandringham,' he said to me and winked. 'No bloody crudités today.'

That Sunday afternoon, after a blissful weekend, Diana and the boys came through to the pantry to say goodbye. Although there was nothing extraordinary about this, I was surprised and troubled by what she said. After thanking Paul and me she took us quietly to one side and continued, 'Whatever happens, I want you to know I have really enjoyed this weekend. It's been very important for me and the boys.' With that she shooed them into the car and drove them back to school.

Paul and I looked at each other after we had waved them off. 'Something's brewing,' he repeated suspiciously. 'And God knows what's going to happen.'

The Prince was still away in Sandringham when the phone rang on the internal line from St James's Palace on Tuesday December 8. It was Lady Jane Strathclyde, the personnel officer, saying she would be coming to Highgrove the following day to tell us in person about an important statement. Jane, normally a gregarious and bubbly character, seemed strangely subdued and would not be drawn further on what the statement was going to reveal. However, Paul and I could guess.

'It's over, Wendy, isn't it?' he said. 'It's finished.' I nodded, but urged him not to say anything to Maria or anyone until we knew for sure. It seemed such a momentous decision to take that I could not quite believe it was happening.

That evening the Highgrove telephone lines were ringing with anxious staff from around the country wanting to find out if we knew the exact wording of the following day's statement. The Palace had wanted to co-ordinate the announcement to staff so that news of the separation would be broken simultaneously to every household. But Jane Strathclyde had still not arrived by the time the Prime Minister, John Major, stood up in the House of Commons to deliver the prepared text.

She did ring, however, to break the news and apologise that she would be late. She told us that the Prime Minister would speak at

3.30pm and that the announcement would be televised, so Paul, Maria, Lita and I waited anxiously in the staff dining room to hear the worst. All of us sat open-mouthed as John Major started to read the statement.

'It is announced from Buckingham Palace that, with regret, The Prince and Princess of Wales have decided to separate. Their Royal Highnesses have no plans to divorce and their constitutional positions are unaffected. This decision has been reached amicably, and they will both continue to participate fully in the upbringing of their children. Their Royal Highnesses will continue to carry out full and separate programmes of public engagements and will, from time to time, attend family occasions and national events together.

'The Queen and the Duke of Edinburgh, though saddened, understand and sympathise with the difficulties that have led to this decision. Her Majesty and His Royal Highness particularly hope that the intrusions into the privacy of The Prince and Princess may now cease. They believe that a degree of privacy and understanding is essential if Their Royal Highnesses are to provide a happy and secure upbringing for their children, while continuing to give a wholehearted commitment to their public duties.'

We sat in stunned silence until I said I needed a cigarette. I was going to go outside, but Maria and Lita joined me at the table as we heard the series of statements by other politicians after the Prime Minister had finished.

Within a few minutes Jane Strathclyde arrived and handed us all a copy of the statement for us to read ourselves. She looked very serious and subdued, and none of us realised at the time what further devastating news she had for us all. She indicated that she wished to speak to Paul and Maria alone. Lita and I went outside, but within seconds we could hear the terrible crying of Maria, obviously distraught by what Jane was telling her.

'I don't want to go back to London,' she sobbed. 'What about our lives? We are all so happy here at Highgrove.' Paul suddenly appeared at the kitchen door. He looked absolutely stunned by the conversation with Jane and said, 'We're not wanted here any more, Wendy. They don't need us any more. Highgrove's going to be shut down and put into mothballs. I simply cannot take it all in at one go.'

It was then my turn to go in and speak with Jane. I passed a still emotional Maria being led into the kitchen by Lita. Jane was distraught, on the verge of tears herself. She had had more than an hour of tears from Maria and looked absolutely drained.

'Wendy, I am very sorry to tell you that you are no longer required at Highgrove. There has been a division of staff, and unfortunately Highgrove will not be used that often by the Prince or Princess. Frances Simpson [the KP housekeeper] will travel with the Prince, since she is no longer required at Kensington Palace, and I'm afraid your job here will no longer exist.'

I did not know how to react, but asked her what was going to happen to the casual staff. Jane told me that they would carry on as normal as and when they were needed, and that the division of staff only affected full-time people. I thanked her, still in a state of shock, and went through to the kitchen to comfort Maria, who was still crying hysterically. 'How can he do this to us?' she screamed. 'Just playing with people's lives. We have made a home for ourselves here and now that is all going to be turned upside down.'

I had been told I would be paid up until July, but that I would have to be out of the Lodge by then. I had spent eight years there and was not looking forward to making another move. Like Maria, I felt slightly bitter that all this had been thrust upon us, and dreaded the upheaval in store. There would not have been any good time for such an announcement, but somehow the fact that it was broken to us just a few weeks before Christmas exacerbated the shock, and plunged us even further into depression.

Yet the façade of togetherness still continued! The next day the Prince and Princess were together at Kensington Palace for the annual Christmas drinks party. And, true to rigid palace etiquette, the subject of the separation was not brought up by either Charles or Diana as they mingled with the dozens of guests. Both smiled nervously as they engaged people in conversation, thanking their staff for their help over the previous year. But as we took the coach home the conversation naturally turned to the changes in store for us all. 'I don't know how they can go through with something like that,' marvelled Paul. 'It just didn't seem real.'

That Christmas was to be my last at Highgrove. The staff party had been organised at a London restaurant, and to my horror I found that I had been seated away from the main room. It was only then that I really understood the enormity of what had happened to me. Because I was due to leave, I had been sidelined – put on a small table in a side room where I could neither see anyone nor hear the speeches. Jane Strathclyde was by my side, but could see how disappointed I was not to be included in the principal party. On my left was the Highgrove orderly, David White, who, trying to be kind, said he felt sorry that I had been left out in the cold. It was difficult to accept what could only be deduced as a snub – and my whole evening was ruined by something as silly as a seating plan. Matters were made worse by Colin Trimming rushing in and telling a policeman at the table that he had managed to get him a place where the action was. I felt desperately miserable, unsure as to why I was being treated so badly. It was the final insult.

1993

CHAPTER NINETEEN

Leaving Highgrove

I was not to see the Princess of Wales until early in the New Year. Diana had decided to spend Christmas with her brother, Earl Spencer, at Althorp in Northamptonshire, and had been forced to give up William and Harry for part of the holiday because Charles wanted them at Sandringham with the Queen. When the Princess did eventually return to Highgrove on a dark, cold evening in early January, it was with her sister Sarah McCorquodale for a late-night raid of a few personal items in her room. Neither woman spoke to anyone that evening, and the visit was kept entirely secret apart from a notification to the police.

They came under cover of darkness and went straight to Diana's sitting room, where the Princess immediately packed up her photo albums, video collection and those pictures small enough to carry back with her in the car. Larger items such as her large charcoal and pencil drawing of an Edwardian lady, various watercolours and drawings of princes William and Harry and Earl Spencer, and several cushions from assorted settees were put to one side ready for collection the following week. Diana left me a note explaining what she had taken, adding that she would be back in a few days for the larger items and several pieces of furniture.

On January 12, having taken William and Harry back to Ludgrove, she arrived shortly after 6pm, with Harold Brown, the KP butler, Paul Burrell, and her favourite interior designer, Dudley Poplak. Her detective Dave Sharp drove down with her, but remained quietly in the kitchen as we walked around the house, taking notes of which things were to go and which to stay.

Diana had brought Dudley because he knew exactly which items belonged to her; which were joint wedding presents; and which were on loan from another royal house. She looked cool and composed as she went around Highgrove, a house she would probably never set foot in again in her life. Her tone was matter-of-fact as she said she 'didn't really care' about most of the things there, and would not keep us long. 'My main concern is for the boys,' she repeated. 'As far as possible I want everything to seem the same when they come here.'

Because of this, and perhaps because it held too many poignant memories, Diana said she did not want to go into the nursery that evening.

'Just leave that as it is, please, Wendy,' she told me. 'I don't want anything changed there at all.'

Dudley looked miserable as we walked around the house. He had designed many of the rooms and was now aware that Charles had asked Robert Kime to redecorate the rooms.

'Don't worry, Dudley. There will be plenty for you to do at Kensington Palace,' said the Princess, taking his arm. 'Now, let's get down to business, shall we?' Every item that she intended to take back to London was written in a ledger book and photographed by Dudley with a polaroid camera. As we walked briskly around the house there were only a few things that Diana seemed adamant about having. 'I've always loved that mirror in the drawing room,' she said to me. 'Let's hope he will let me have that.' There was a table that had come with her from Althorp but she decided to leave that for the boys as well. In fact, in an hour she had accumulated very little, choosing only to take a few vases and some cheap furniture that she had brought over from her flat in Coleherne Court before her marriage. 'Now, nobody can accuse me of stripping the place bare, can they?' she laughed lightly as we all went upstairs.

Diana paused briefly before going into her room, and took a deep breath. In the bright electric light she looked around her, trying to remain detached and as unemotional as possible. Her eyes, however, betrayed her, and all of us knew she was choked with emotion.

'I'll take all those, please,' she said quietly to Dudley, pointing to the various photographs and pictures on her bathroom wall. 'They are not valuable but just personal things that he won't miss.' Snapshots of Diana and the boys along with professional portraits of her around the world were taken off the walls by Paul and Ken as she walked through into the corridor. 'Helena will come for my clothes,' she told me. 'Don't worry about doing any of that yourself, Wendy.'

As we walked downstairs I said how sorry I was about the separation. The Princess stopped briefly, then, looking me straight in the eye, said: 'Don't be sorry, Wendy. It's all for the best in the long term, as I'm sure you know.' She added: 'It's been very hard but everything will turn out to be much better for the boys in the end.' The Princess said we would see each other soon in London, and walked through to her sitting room to wait for Paul and Harold to finish packing her car.

The drawing room, previously decorated by Dudley Poplak, had been redone by Robert Kime, and Dudley asked if he could have a look at it. 'Yes, I can see what's happening here,' he murmured as I switched on the lamps. 'You can see this is an old man's room now. The Prince is withdrawing into the womb. It's just like one of those rooms at Sandringham. You can see how he's regressing to childhood, what he was brought up with.' Dudley tutted quietly to himself, as he looked at the new red curtains, a tapestry-covered sofa and a marble-topped side table. Robert Kime, who had worked on the room for several months, had left the original light green walls but changed the carpet from green to a hessian basket-weave.

'This room used to be so light and airy,' Dudley said. 'Now it's heavy and so suppressed.' I turned off the lamps and accompanied him down the passageway. 'It's very sad, isn't it?' he said, gesturing towards the sitting room where Diana was waiting. 'But she's being incredibly strong about things. I just hope she can maintain that fantastic composure.'

I thought about what the Princess had told me as she pulled away in her car, taking the back drive exit rather than the front to avoid anyone seeing her. Her comment that it was perhaps 'for the best' seemed right the more I thought about it, especially as far as William and Harry were concerned. I think she realised that eventually both children would have been irredeemably scarred by the continual tension and acrimony of her relationship with the Prince. And I think also she was beginning to recognise that, in the past, she had been less than fair in the matter of Charles's access to his sons.

'I suppose there will be a straightforward division of time spent with the boys,' said Paul as he locked the front door. 'But you can bet anything you like the Prince will want legal custody.' Both of us walked back to the kitchen for one last cup of tea together. 'What are you going to do, Wendy?' he asked. I told him I would be paid up until July but that after that I had no idea what was going to happen.

Paul and Maria had been asked to go and work for the Princess at Kensington Palace, and would be moving later that spring. 'They haven't treated you at all well, have they?' said Paul sympathetically. 'You know that Maria and I will always be there for you if you need us.' I thanked him for all his kindness, and wondered what was going to happen to Highgrove, in the light of Jane Strathclyde's comment that much of it was not going to be used any more.

But as I found out that Friday, when she came to sort out my pension arrangements, much of what she had said had been misleading. Far from being closed down, it was merely undergoing a radical redecoration, and a clear-out of staff. 'I'm sorry, Wendy, but I was told initially that the Prince would not be spending nearly as much time here,' she told me that afternoon. 'Now, however, it looks as if he has changed his mind, and as you know there is nothing new in that.' She looked at me and laughed nervously. 'There will be lots of changes around here and we wondered if you would like to work up to April, then vacate the Lodge with a lump sum of six months' money.' She added: 'I should take it if I were you, because by law we only have to give you one month's notice.'

I thanked her and asked if she would give me a few days to think about what I was going to do. But in the meantime I said I would stay at the Lodge and continue to work as housekeeper, at least until they found a replacement for me. As I went down the main drive to the Lodge that evening I felt great waves of anger. I didn't blame Jane, because she was not capable of lying, but I did feel almost cheated. Why couldn't they have told me the truth in the first place? I thought to myself. Why bother saying the house was closing down when it wasn't? I decided to stay until April, then take the lump-sum offer.

.   .   .

On Thursday January 28 the Prince returned to Highgrove, and walked through the front door as if nothing had changed in his life. He seemed buoyant and chatty, saying how glad he was to be back and asking if

I had had a good Christmas. Nothing was said about my having to leave, and the Prince obviously felt confident that I would not mention it to him. Earlier that day I had been sent a fax from his new rooms at St James's Palace listing the dates he would be spending at Highgrove over the next few months. The list showed that, far from leaving the house in mothballs, Charles was intending to spend more time there than ever.

William and Harry were due to spend their first exeat with their father, but not at Highgrove. Charles took Tigger and Roo with him, picking up the boys from school and then departing for a secret destination. Paul said he had heard from the Princess that Charles had taken them to somewhere in Norfolk and that Camilla had been in the house party.

'Nothing surprises me any more about that man,' said Paul bitterly as he came to collect his personal things from the pantry. 'In the light of what has happened I simply cannot believe he has the nerve to do something like that.' Paul was talking about the recent newspaper revelations of a taped conversation between the Prince and Camilla Parker Bowles, which provided evidence of an affair between them. During the conversation the Prince and Camilla discussed secret rendezvous and talked explicitly about their lovemaking. The disclosures seemed to do little to embarrass the Prince, who seemed as cheerful and resilient as ever.

The only effect the 'Camillagate' tape had on him was a tightening up of telephone security at Highgrove. On Tuesday February 2, British Telecom came to put another private, secret line in the main bedroom, which was being permanently used by Charles now that the Princess had moved out. Despite all the previous publicity they did not have the correct wiring, however, which led to a stern rebuke from Michael Fawcett, the Prince's valet. 'They knew exactly what they had to do with the scrambler phone, yet couldn't even get the right wires here,' he cursed to me that evening. 'No wonder we have had all these terrible breaches of security.'

. . .

Paul and Maria, meanwhile, had gone down to London to join the Princess, their departure from Highgrove treated with the utmost glee by the Prince. Paul had gone through to the Prince's study to say goodbye, and had been terribly upset by Charles's reaction. Apparently the Prince had barely looked up. 'Are you really surprised?' said

Michael the following day as I told him how upset Paul had been. 'The Prince knew how close Paul and Maria were to the Princess, and knew they were on her side. He could see them chatting conspiratorially to her whenever his back was turned. When I originally asked him what was going to happen to the Burrells the Prince replied, "Who cares? I don't want people like that running around at Highgrove."'

The Princess threw a drinks party on Thursday February 4 at her apartments at Kensington Palace. I asked Charles's permission to attend, even though I was meant to be on duty at Highgrove, and he scrawled 'approved' on the note I had left out for him.

That evening Diana was surrounded by friends and seemed bright and happy as she discussed where her work was going to take her over the next few months. She seemed concerned about me and asked if I had found somewhere to go, looking worried when I told her I did not have any plans. The whole affair was informal and relaxed, completely different from the more regimented party given by Charles for Paddy Whiteland's eightieth birthday the following evening. The Prince, who counted Paddy as one of his longest-serving and most faithful servants, had allowed the drinks party to be held in the hall at Highgrove, but had said to me that he wanted everyone out within a couple of hours. 'We don't want everyone hanging around all night, do we?' he said rather dismissively as he went up to his room to bathe. 'And anyway I am having the P-Ts round for dinner, so I want to have the house cleared by then.'

For someone as otherwise fastidious, the Prince of Wales had a very earthy sense of humour, something he had obviously inherited from his father. The following evening he took Paddy to a private Beauvoir Hunt supper and was presented with a fox's penis bone mounted on a silver pin. The Prince loved the gift, a traditional fertility symbol, and pinned it to his lapel that Sunday as he waited for the King of Greece to arrive.

King Constantine and Charles carefully inspected the present as they took drinks in the sitting room that evening, swapping lewd jokes about how much they could do with some good luck in that department. The Prince, who had a fascination generally with bodily functions, and like Fergie loved a good fart joke, wore the pin quite often until it was packed away by a quick-thinking valet who was worried about how insensitive a public wearing of the gift might seem in the light of the recent marriage break-up.

The Prince's friends were concerned at how he was coping with all the publicity about the separation, but they need not have worried. Rarely had I seen Charles so relaxed and carefree. The fact that his estrangement from Diana was now public allowed him to breathe again in his own house, content that the Princess was not likely to appear unannounced and upset his routine. Naturally, nothing was ever said by Charles about the events of the last few months, but there was a certain optimism in his mood that suggested he had now got over the shock of Diana's betrayal and the worst of the publicity.

The redecoration of Highgrove continued apace and there were daily visits from Robert Kime, who organised regular deliveries of furniture from the Buckingham Palace store and other royal residences for the Prince to consider. The bookshelves in the Princess's sitting room were ripped out and the walls stripped of any traces of Diana's influence. It looked very much as if the Prince was purging himself of all traces of his wife, giving himself and Highgrove a new start after so many years of unhappiness.

The clear-out also extended to the store-rooms and basements, which had gradually filled with official presents and other gifts sent to the royal couple since the last sort-out. 'Burn it all,' said Paddy as he struggled to dump a finely carved wooden rocking horse in the incinerator at the back of the house. 'Those were my orders.' I watched in horror as piles of beautifully made pieces of furniture were lobbed into the flames, along with the standard teddy bears and toys sent in from royal fans around the world for William and Harry. 'You start royal service as a monarchist but very quickly become a republican,' Paul had once told me. And he was right. It made me angry to see so many gifts and clothes go up in smoke, when so much could have been given away to charity or to the homeless.

The following week took the Prince on a solo visit to America, where he was amazed and excited by his rapturous reception from the thousands of people who turned out to see him. While he was away, British Telecom came back to install yet more lines in the library and to fit another 'secrecy' phone in the Prince's bedroom. These phones were theoretically impossible to tap or intercept. The Prince was adamant that he wanted these and not just normal land lines after the Camillagate saga. The phones travelled with Charles in a large case when he was in this country, and could be plugged into certain wall sockets.

The fact that the Prince had waited for Diana to leave before making these changes seemed perverse to us all. If he had taken such care in previous years, none of the tapes could have been made. Charles, despite being a Colonel-in-Chief of several regiments and a reasonably intelligent man, had no idea about personal security, needing constant reminders from his personal staff about the most basic areas. The newspapers had been full of royal bugging stories for weeks, and, even in the fall-out from the tape scandals, Charles was surprised when it was suggested his personal rooms should be swept for listening devices. In the last few weeks everyone had been under suspicion, getting late-night visits from royal protection squad officers asking us if we knew anything about who was behind the recent revelations.

Diana's personal line was cut off at Highgrove on the Prince's orders, and after that there was very little evidence left of the Princess of Wales at the house. Her presence finally extinguished, Charles settled down to entertain his close circle of friends for weekend house parties and small dinner parties. Larger Duchy lunches for fourteen or more people were juggled with visits from the Prince's advisers including Jonathan Porritt, Professor Norman Myers and Sir Laurens Van der Post.

Camilla Parker Bowles was not on the guest list, and nobody was able to work out if he was still seeing her in private. We were convinced that Charles was incapable of breaking off all contact, and were intrigued as to what was happening with their relationship. My hunch was that they were still speaking regularly on the secrecy phones, especially during the long Sunday evenings at Highgrove when the Prince would retire into his library for hours on end.

On March 12, with the house almost finished, Emilie Van Cutsem arrived for the weekend. She found the new rooms very exciting and wandered around upstairs, marvelling at the Prince's good taste. Mrs Van Cutsem was waiting for her son Edward to arrive by train from Durham University, both of them having been invited by the Prince to spend the weekend with him, William and Harry. 'The poor boys,' said Emilie conspiratorially to me. 'They must have been through so much.'

Edward Van Cutsem was by now in his late teens, and had worked for a spell in the office at Buckingham Palace between school and university. The Prince liked him, and enjoyed having him around when the boys were at home. 'Edward is so good with the young Princes,' cooed Mrs Van Cutsem, who now seemed to be taking on something of a maternal role in the boys' upbringing. 'He gives them someone to look up to as a role model.' She had brought her son's gun with her and that weekend Edward, William and Harry went out together to shoot rabbits. They came back late that Saturday afternoon with at least a dozen, and William and Harry excitedly recounted how they had both shot one each. Charles looked on contentedly and asked for exact details of where and how they had made the kills.

The next day both boys went out all morning with Edward for another shooting expedition. Unfortunately, I very nearly got caught in the crossfire. As I was walking back to the Lodge after clearing up the breakfast things, I heard a shot go off above my head. Darting for cover, I came across the Prince walking around the side of the house with Emilie Van Cutsem. Chuckling at the near miss, he strode purposefully around to the front of the house and shouted: 'Hold your fire, men. Wendy wants to get home.'

'No,' shrieked William, in fits of laughter. 'Not until a forfeit's been paid.'

'I'm out of money but I will pay later,' I shouted back, letting the Prince walk me gingerly down the drive. 'Bloody hooligans,' he laughed. 'Well, at least take some comfort from the fact that they will get me as well as you if they start taking potshots.'

Neither child mentioned their mother once that weekend and seemed perfectly contented to join in with the Prince and his party, which included the Palmer-Tomkinsons. Emilie Van Cutsem seemed surprised at how resilient they were, and said cosily to me, 'I think things will really work out for them. They don't seem at all affected by everything, thank God.'

It was to be my last week at work, and with the Prince going abroad that Monday afternoon, time to say goodbye. I was walking through to the library with his snack bag of orange, milk and cream, bags of wheatgerm, linseed, prunes and sultanas, which he would take with him on the way to the airport, when suddenly Paddy burst into the room in front of me. There had been another disaster. Prince Harry's pony had just broken his leg in the paddock and would need to be destroyed.

'Oh, God,' said the Prince. 'There's always something dying on me,' before seeing him out of the room. Then, going over to his desk, he produced a leather-bound photograph of himself and a small silver box embossed with the Prince of Wales feathers, and held out his hand.

Standing there in his uniform, with his blue eyes shining and his teeth flashing white, he went through the same speech that he must have made on hundreds of such occasions.

'Thank you so much, Wendy, for all your hard work,' he said with a smile. 'I know this is not very much of a parting present, but I want you to know how much I have appreciated having you here at Highgrove. I will miss you very much.' We spoke for a few minutes about my family and what plans I had in store for the future, before Michael came in to say it was time for him to leave. 'Do come back to see us at St James's whenever you want,' said Charles with a smile. 'You will always be welcome.' And with that he walked out to the car.

. . .

The following Friday I went into the house for one last time to say goodbye to the staff. Mrs Van Cutsem had arrived for the weekend, and after saying farewell to her I joined Chris and the others in the dining room for bottles of wine and champagne. I looked around the room, at the policemen and the valets who had been part of my life for so many years, and felt quite overcome with emotion. Despite all the upheavals and traumas, all the rows and petty jealousies, I was sorry to be leaving. A group of us walked down to the Lodge, where we continued the party until dawn.

The Princess rang several days later to invite me for a farewell lunch at San Lorenzo, her favourite London restaurant. Meeting for drinks at Kensington Palace shortly after midday on Monday April 26, about ten of us then took cars down to the restaurant at Beauchamp Place and were astonished to see that we had been given a private room upstairs. 'Look at you! So thin!' said the Italian owner, the kindly and talkative Mara Berni, as she pinched Diana's arm. 'Now, what are you going to eat?'

Ken Wharfe was there, as were Mervyn Wycherly, Paul and Maria, and Helena, the dresser. A group of people from the office filled the rest of the places around the large table, with me at the centre and the Princess to my left. Paul seemed on edge that day, whispering conspiratorially to me that the Princess was not speaking to him any more, as we took our places. But as far as I was concerned she seemed on tremendous form, laughing and joking with Ken and filling me in on all the latest household gossip.

. . .

Diana's staff had taken great care to organise the lunch, but as we were running out of time the Princess decided to skip the main course of veal and move straight from the pasta starter to the pudding. As a result there was no main course for anyone, since everyone traditionally kept pace with the her.

Finally it was time for coffee, and at that moment a specially made cake was brought out, and bottles of champagne opened. The Princess, giggling at something Ken had just said, got up to thank me, handing me a small enamel box and a signed picture of herself. 'For your collection,' she laughed, before whispering quietly into my ear, 'as you go out into the real world.'

Diana and her female detective left a few minutes later for an appointment, leaving the rest of us to carry on enjoying ourselves at the restaurant. Some of the company broke into song as the day wore on. Ken and the other policemen talked candidly about how life had changed since the separation. 'Well, she seems to have started to get what she wants,' said one of them, talking about the Princess. 'Yes,' agreed Ken, his florid complexion deepening with the wine. 'But where is it all going to end?'